W9-BER-135

Praise for Walter Dean Myers's

Malcolm X
By Any Means Necessary

★ "Myers shapes the information on Malcolm X with a consistent, well-supported argument as to what determined the course of his subject's life."
—*The Bulletin of the Center for Children's Books*, STARRED REVIEW

★ "Incisive, precise prose…[a] carefully researched portrait of a deeply devoted individual." —*Publishers Weekly*, STARRED REVIEW

"Myers's biography pays eloquent tribute to the brilliant, radical African American leader…passages of quiet intensity capture the essence of the man." —*Booklist*, BOXED REVIEW

"If one can choose only one book about Malcolm X this is the book of choice." —*Voice of Youth Advocates*

"The author has done a fine job of introducing the reader to Malcolm X…. The book presents exciting material…. An excellent choice for any school or home library." —*The Horn Book Magazine*

"[Myers] strikes a good balance between his subject's personal life and broader social issues and movements…. [His] evenhanded approach will provoke thought and discussion among reluctant readers."
—*School Library Journal*

"A sensitive and objective account of the controversial activist." —*Essence*

"A fervent portrait of the controversial man…. [S]teer readers to Myers for a sense of the rage and frustration that fueled Malcolm X's brief career."
—*Kirkus Reviews*

A Coretta Scott King Honor Book
An ALA Notable Children's Book
A *Horn Book* Fanfare Book
A Notable Children's Trade Book
   in the Field of Social Studies

A new direction in nonfiction.

POLARIS

We Shall Not Be Moved
The Women's Factory Strike of 1909
BY JOAN DASH

An American Hero
The True Story of Charles A. Lindbergh
BY BARRY DENENBERG

Winning Ways
A Photohistory of American Women in Sports
BY SUE MACY

Malcolm X

By Any Means Necessary

Walter Dean Myers

SCHOLASTIC INC.   NEW YORK · TORONTO · LONDON · AUCKLAND · SYDNEY

Excerpts from *The Autobiography of Malcolm X*, by Malcolm X, with the assistance of Alex Haley. Copyright © 1964 by Alex Haley and Malcolm X. Copyright © 1965 by Alex Haley and Betty Shabazz. Reprinted by permission of Random House Inc.

Excerpts from *Malcolm X Speaks*, copyright © 1965 by Betty Shabazz and Pathfinder Press. All rights reserved. Reprinted by permission of Pathfinder Press.

"Great Bateleur" is used by permission of Wopashitwe Mondo Eyen we Langa.

Cover photo: © John Launois/Black Star.

No part of this publication may be reproduced in whole or in part, or stored in a retrieval system, or transmitted in any form or by any means, electronic, mechanical, photocopying, recording, or otherwise, without written permission of the publisher. For information regarding permission, write to Scholastic Inc., 555 Broadway, New York, NY 10012.

ISBN 0-590-29912-3

Copyright © 1993 by Walter Dean Myers. All rights reserved. Published by Scholastic Inc. POLARIS, SCHOLASTIC, and associated logos are trademarks and/or registered trademarks of Scholastic Inc.

12 11 10 9 8 7 6 5 4 3 2 1   1   8 9/9 0 1 2 3/0

Printed in the U.S.A.   23

To the Harlem Writers Guild

Contents

Preface

◆————————————◆

THE SIXTIES was a decade of change in the United States. Some of the changes were orderly, some were not. In a way it was the first period in American history in which people took their protests to the streets and actually forced changes in the way the country went about its business. The changes began, as so many do, with a people's protesting against a long-standing injustice, in this case the evils of a racially divided society.

From the hard times of the civil rights movement, from the jails and the bombings, the hatred and the love, the curses and the prayers, emerged some of the most memorable people in the history of this country: people such as Martin Luther King, Jr., Thurgood Marshall, Medgar Evers, Fannie Lou Hamer, Septima Clark, and the Kennedy brothers, Robert and John. There were people who were quietly courageous, who risked their lives for their fellow human beings, and who far too often lost their lives. Not since the Civil War had there been as much violence on American streets.

It is hard now to think of a United States in which black people could not even drink from the same water fountains as white people, or in which black students could not attend public schools that their tax dollars had paid for, simply because of the color of their skin. In some places, blacks were barred from restaurants, prevented from voting, and forced to sit in the backs of buses. To be black was to be treated with contempt, a contempt that was often backed by what were then called "Jim Crow" laws. In the wrenching days of protest known as the civil rights movement, America confronted its racial problems, not only in the courts, but in the streets as well. It is a rare testimony to the American system of government that the country was not torn apart.

To select one person, or even one group of people, as being pivotal to the sixties is risky. There were many people who were important in that exciting time in American history. Who is best remembered? Whose words have best stood the test of time? Whose actions most defined the temper of the times as we remember that time, and that temper, from the present? For many it was a man named Malcolm X.

It was Malcolm's anger, his biting wit, his dedication, that put the hard edge on the movement, that provided the other side of the sword, not the handle of acceptance and nonviolence, but the blade.

"Whoever heard of a nonviolent revolution?" Malcolm

asked. "Whoever heard of a revolution without bloodshed?"

The mere possibilities inherent in the questions sent government officials to back-room planning strategies with nonviolent demonstrators.

Malcolm showed that one person, riding the crest of social discontent, could still inspire great masses of people. He displayed the awesome potential of a portion of black America that many thought would sleep forever and proved that black docility was a thing of the past. Malcolm and the Nation of Islam drove the civil rights movement, gave it the dark side that many feared it might have. It was Malcolm who said to black Americans that they did not always have to hide their pain, or their outrage. It was Malcolm who claimed the imagination of young black men as no one had since Frederick Douglass had called them to fight in the Civil War.

The segregation signs have been taken down now. They can be bought at flea markets as "collectibles" from a distant era. The pictures of black students being escorted to school by armed soldiers can be found only in history books. But the memories of the sixties, and of Malcolm X, remain. He remains because he represented, and still represents, something that other leaders, leaders as courageous as Malcolm, did not. These leaders, black and white, men and women, willing to risk their lives in the search for justice for all people, represented a courage that was right for the time. But Malcolm's words speak to today's time, and to the young people of today who, in many ways, are as different from the mainstream of American life in the nineties as their parents were in the fifties and sixties. The reasons might be different, but the disillusionment is the same.

Malcolm scared America. The fear he generated might well have cost him his life. But in scaring America, in bringing it face-to-face with the realities of our society in the sixties, he left it a better place.

Introduction:
A Man Called
Malcolm

A PRIL, 1957, New York City. Two black-and-white New York City police cars pulled up to the curb in front of the 28th Precinct. Curious onlookers watched as the police pulled a black man from the back of one of the cars. The man's arms were handcuffed behind him. There was blood on his head and on the front of his shirt.

Two hefty police officers, one on either side, half lifted, half pulled the man into the station. On the street some people commented to each other and then went about their business. It wasn't the first time that a black man had been hauled into the police station, or even the first time one had been brought into the station bleeding.

One Hundred and Twenty-third Street is in the center of Harlem. The street is not particularly wide, and often the police cars in front of the precinct were parked on the sidewalk. Red and brown buildings along the street, which had seemed almost colorless during the long winter months, were coming alive in the early spring weather. Already there were signs of the coming summer.

On the fire escapes overlooking the street were flower boxes, an occasional mop put out to dry, and sometimes a small child playing under the watchful eye of a grandparent. In the windows the serious watchers, the women who brought special pillows to the windows on which to rest their elbows, didn't spend much time on precinct activity. There were other, more cheerful things to see on the busy street. There were always the children, playing spirited games of ring-o-leevio and stickball, moving reluctantly from their games to allow cars to pass. Older women sat in front of their homes and exchanged the most recent gossip. Old men played bid whist or dominoes while young men whispered their best lines to slim-waisted girls.

The street held a rich assortment of colors. The brightly colored skirts of Jamaican blacks, the white shirts of the old men, and the blue jeans of the youngest boys all served to offset the drabness of the buildings themselves. But the most vibrant colors were those of the inhabitants of the street. They ranged from the deep brown, almost pure black, of some of the boys idly bouncing a basketball, to the cinnamon-colored shopkeeper on the corner, to the cream-colored, almost white, woman playing with her child.

The baseball season had just started and there was talk about the retirement of Jackie Robinson. Jackie had been a Harlem hero from his entrance into professional baseball in 1947 until he had decided to hang up his spikes.

Some old-timers were talking about the ballplayers from the old Negro Leagues: Cool Papa Bell, Josh Gibson, and Buck Leonard. Younger men were talking about Willie Mays.

Suddenly there was a stirring on the street; something was happening. There is an unspoken language in Harlem, a way that the people walk, and look at one another, that signals that something important is going on. The casual pace is suddenly quickened, the rhythms of the street are less relaxed, there is an electricity in the air. There was a decrease in the volume of street noises. Portable radios were turned down, conversations were interrupted. Eyes turned toward the busy 28th Precinct. What they saw shocked them.

In front of the 28th Precinct was a formation of black men. They were all dressed neatly with short haircuts, their arms folded before them. Some wore dark glasses, many wore suits. None of them were smiling.

"The Black Muslims!"

The word quickly spread along the street. The women in the windows shifted the pillows that protected their elbows from the concrete windowsills. A crowd began to gather around the men in formation. A white policeman took a look at the lines of men and quickly disappeared into the station house.

A brown-skinned young man, tall and blade-thin, carefully surveyed the formation that defiantly faced the precinct doors. Pleased by what he saw, he adjusted his glasses, walked toward the station house, and through the heavy doors.

Inside the station the young man walked quickly to the desk sergeant. He noticed the white police officers gathered at the windows.

The thin man who confronted the desk sergeant demanded to see the black man who earlier had been brought to the station bleeding and in cuffs. He asked for the man by name.

The officer at the desk said that the man wasn't there, but the stern-faced man in front of him insisted that he was. The officer seemed nervous as he admitted that the man was indeed there, but that he could not be seen.

"And who are you?" the officer asked.

"Malcolm X!" The answer was quick in coming, and forcefully delivered.

Malcolm X declared that until the man, Johnson Hinton, was actually seen, and he was personally assured of Hinton's safety and that he was receiving proper medical attention, the formation that had assembled outside the precinct would remain.

The police of the 28th Precinct had heard of the militant group commonly called the Black Muslims, but they had never seen it represented in this manner. The entire scene looked like trouble.

In Harlem the police did what they felt was necessary

to maintain law and order. There had been occasional difficulties, but never an organized group of black men as this seemed to be. It was said that the Black Muslims hated all whites and were trained in the martial arts.

The desk officer relented and allowed the man before him, Malcolm X, to see the man the police had arrested earlier.

"That man belongs in the hospital," Malcolm announced.

An ambulance was called, and Johnson Hinton was taken to Harlem Hospital. The men who had formed ranks outside of the police station remained in formation as they followed the route of the ambulance to the hospital on Lenox Avenue. The crowd following the small force of men grew as they passed through the streets. By the time they had reached Harlem Hospital the crowd had grown sufficiently for the local police to contact police headquarters in lower Manhattan.

A police official approached Malcolm X and told him bluntly that he would have to move his people away from the hospital.

Malcolm refused, saying that the members of the Nation of Islam were standing peacefully, within their constitutional rights, and harming no one. The police officer looked at the men standing in ranks, and walked away. Malcolm sent one of the men into the hospital to check on the condition of Hinton.

The crowd behind the formation was growing more restless and more police were summoned. Soon there were two lines of men facing each other, one white, the other black. The policemen were not sure of what was happening. The men of the Nation of Islam were motionless.

The police official returned to Malcolm and told him that the crowd behind his formation was shouting at the police and acting in a manner that he could not tolerate.

Malcolm said that he would control the members of the Nation of Islam, and that the rest of the crowd was the problem of the police official. Again, the police official backed off.

The man that Malcolm had sent into the hospital returned. He told Malcolm the doctors had assured him that Hinton was getting the best care possible. Malcolm signaled the formation of men and they moved silently away.

That night and the next morning the community was filled with talk of "the Muslims," and how they had confronted the police. The police talked about the incident as well and wondered exactly what challenge the Muslims presented to them and exactly who was this man who called himself Malcolm X.

1

---◆---

The Father

PEOPLE do not just "happen" in history. They come along at a certain time, and in a certain place. They react to ideas that have come before them, and to people who have expressed those ideas. The man we know as Malcolm X was no exception. To understand who Malcolm was, there is no better place to begin than with his father.

His family name was Little, but Malcolm's father, Earl, was a big man. Tall, heavyset, and dark, he was a man capable of working with his hands and with his mind. But in Reynolds, Georgia, where the Littles lived, there were few opportunities for black men. Earl Little knew what he wanted to do with his life: to help his people gain their independence, and to help African-Americans everywhere to reach their full potential. He also wanted a family, but his first marriage did not work out and left him still searching for the settled life he so badly wanted.

Although his family still lived in Reynolds, Earl decided to continue his travels, eventually finding his way to Montreal, Canada. It was in Montreal that he met Louise Norton, an attractive black woman who had come to Canada from the British island of Grenada. Earl soon fell in love with Louise and proposed marriage. In 1919 the couple was married and settled in Philadelphia.

The year the Littles were married was a year of difficulties for African-Americans. Many had believed that since they had fought for America in what had been described as the "war to end all wars," World War I, they would not face the same kind of racism they had before the war had started. They were wrong. Black American soldiers had received international attention in Europe for their valor and bravery and had received medals and honors for their participation in the First World War. But neither recognition for their sacrifices nor their bravery made a difference back home in the United States.

In the States, people of color were not given the same rights as were given to whites. In many parts of the country, north and south, black people could not live in white neighborhoods, go to schools with whites, ride in the same railroad cars, play in the same public parks, or even drink

Malcolm's parents, Louise and Earl Little

from the same water fountains. In some parts of the country this separation of the races, called segregation, was legal. In other parts of the country segregation was not legal, but blacks were still forced to accept the role of second-class citizens. They found that law officials would not protect them when they tried to put a stop to these practices.

More important, many blacks were the victims of mob violence that ranged from being beaten to actually being killed. Some blacks who had been accused of crimes against whites were hung by white mobs without the benefit of trials or any legal proceedings. Others were beaten or killed just because they had angered some white person. The law did very little to protect these people.

In the year that Earl Little married Louise Norton, there were a number of lynchings across the United States. One of them happened in Omaha, Nebraska. A man named Will Brown was accused of attacking a white woman. He was put in jail while the charges were being investigated. A large gang of young white men stormed the jail, demanding that the prisoner be turned over to them to be killed. The sheriff refused, saying that the prisoner should be given a fair trial. The mob, which grew larger by the hour, set fire to the jail, threatening the lives of the other prisoners and the guards as well. They shot the town's mayor when he tried to intervene in the lawless act.

After a long siege in which many people were injured and killed, the prisoner was handed over and immediately shot by the rioters. He was then hung from a utility pole while members of the crowd fired more shots at him.

Over the following days the newspapers in Omaha were filled with stories of people who thought that this illegal act had been the right thing to do. This was the world that Earl and Louise Little faced as they began their married life. Indeed, it was the world that all African-Americans faced.

But Earl Little did not simply accept this world; he tried to change it. In the first days of his marriage to Louise, when the couple was in Philadelphia, Earl had heard the speeches of a fiery black leader named Marcus Garvey. To the Littles, Garvey's ideas were not merely appealing, they were electrifying.

**Marcus Garvey, the founder of
the Universal Negro Improvement Association**

Marcus Garvey, like Louise Little, was born in the British West Indies. Garvey was born in 1887, on the island of Jamaica. It was clear to Garvey that black people all over the world were not doing well. In Jamaica, a largely black population was, with few exceptions, living in poverty. Blacks in the United States were on the bottom of the economic ladder, and the rich resources of Africa were being exploited by European and North American companies. Garvey believed that African-Americans were too dependent on whites. They needed to create their own businesses, their own jobs, and their own schools if they wanted to succeed in the world. They also needed a spiritual home, he thought, and what better home for African-Americans than Africa?

Garvey had created the U.N.I.A., the Universal Negro Improvement Association, and a newspaper, *Negro World*.

When Earl Little moved his family to Omaha, Nebraska, he took the ideas of Marcus Garvey with him. Garvey needed good people to help spread his message, and Earl Little soon became the head of the Omaha chapter of the U.N.I.A.

Life was tough for the Littles in Omaha. Blacks were the last ones hired for the few available jobs, and the first ones fired when work was slow. Many of the men in the small city worked on seasonal jobs, and the women were lucky if they could get jobs cleaning the homes of the whites in the area.

The Little family grew. Earl and Louise had had three children by the time they arrived in Omaha in 1925. On the nineteenth of May of that year they had their fourth child, a boy they named Malcolm.

Earl Little understood that the church gave blacks the opportunity to worship, but also to organize. The city directory of Omaha, in 1926, listed him only as a laborer, but to his people, he was a man of ideas.

Elder Little, as he was known, was an excellent speaker. As a minister he delivered the message of Christian salvation, but it was his political talks that brought him the most attention among both blacks and whites. He spoke of the problems of the black race, and the ideas and philosophy of Marcus Garvey. It was not a message that went over well in a city in which blacks were not supposed to

Omaha-Douglas County Health Department

1. PLACE OF BIRTH

Division of Vital Statistics

Certificate # A39357

County ____Douglas____

Township _____

CERTIFICATE OF BIRTH

City ____Omaha____ Street ____University Hospital____

2. FULL NAME OF CHILD ____Malcolm Little____

3. Sex. male	If Plural Births	4. Twin, triplet, or other _____ 5. Number, in order of birth _____	6. Premature _____ Full term _____	7. Date of birth ____May 19____ 19__25

8. Full Name FATHER ____Earley Little____	17. Full Maiden Name MOTHER ____Louise Norton____
9. Post Office ____3448 Pinkney St.____	18. Post Office ____same____
10. Color or race ____Negro____ 11. Age last birthday ____35____ (Years)	19. Color or race ____Negro____ 20. Age last birthday ____28____ (Years)
12. Birthplace (city or place) ____Georgia____ (State or country)	21. Birthplace (city or place) ____West Indies (Br)____ (State or Country)
13. Trade, profession or particular kind of work done, as spinner, sawyer, bookkeeper, etc. ____Laborer____	22. Trade, profession, or particular kind of work done, as housekeeper, typist, nurse, clerk, etc. ____hwf____
14. Industry or business in which work was done, as silk mill, saw mill, bank, etc.	23. Industry or business in which work was done, as own home, lawyer's office, silk mill, etc.
15. Date (Mo. and Yr.) last engaged in this work _____19____ 16. Total time (years) spent in this work _____	OCCUPATION	24. Date (Mo. and Yr.) last engaged in this work _____19____ 25. Total time (years) spent in the work _____

26. Number of children of this mother (at time of this birth, and including this child. (a) Born alive and now living ____4____ (b) Born alive but now dead _____ (c) Stillborn _____

27. If stillborn, period of gestation _____ months or weeks, 28. Cause of still birth _____ { Before labor _____ During labor _____

CERTIFICATE OF ATTENDING PHYSICIAN*

I hereby certify that I attended the birth of this child, who was ____alive____ at ____10:25____
(Born alive) (Stillborn)
on the date above stated.

*When no physician is in attendance certificate shall be completed and signed by the parent or other person present.

Signature ____W. D. Lear____ M.D.

STATE LAW

Address ____University Hospital____

Was silver solution instilled in each eye? ____yes____

Filed with local registrar ____5-26-25____ Date

____A. S. Pinto____ Registrar

I hereby certify that the above is a true and correct copy of the certificate of birth recorded in the City of Omaha, County of Douglas, State of Nebraska.

Dated this ____20th____ day of ____May____, 19__68__

____DD Lyman M.D.____ Registrar

Malcolm X's birth certificate

13

speak out or to stand up for their rights. Nervous blacks discouraged Elder Little from talking about the rights of black people. They were afraid he would just stir up trouble for them. The Ku Klux Klan, a white hate group, was also active in Omaha, and they warned Elder Little to keep his mouth shut about what the black man should do in Omaha.

Women were encouraged to become active members of the U.N.I.A., and Louise Little also joined the militant

OMAHA, NEB.

——————◆——————

The Omaha Division met on Sunday, June 13, in Liberty Hall, 2528 Lake street The president, Mr. E. Little, presiding. Opening song from "Greenland's Icy Mountains." Prayer and preamble by the president. Musical selection. Prof. A. Vance was introduced and held his hearers' attention about matters of the organization. A membership drive was launched for the coming week, in which Mr. Vance will participate.

LOUISE LITTLE, Reporter.

Louise Little reported on the activities of the U.N.I.A.'s Omaha chapter.

organization, reporting the activities of the Omaha chapter to the national U.N.I.A. office in New York's Harlem.

Often the meetings, held on Lake Street in Omaha, in the center of the black community, would begin with the singing of the hymn "From Greenland's Icy Mountains."

> *From Greenland's icy mountains*
> *From India's coral strand*
> *Where Afric's sunny fountains*
> *Roll down their golden sand*
> *From many an ancient river*
> *From many a palmy plain*
> *They call us to deliver*
> *Their land from Error's chain.*

As Elder Little continued to speak out for the rights of his people, he gained more and more attention in Omaha, and received more and more threats from white racists. The racists could force Elder Little to move by threatening the safety of his family, and by threatening those in Omaha who employed him. It was after a particularly frightening threat that Earl Little moved his family from Omaha to Milwaukee, Wisconsin.

Although he had moved from Omaha, Earl Little did not move away from his faith in spreading the message of black independence, gaining more and more respect within the U.N.I.A. as a speaker and as a religious leader. When the Little family moved to Milwaukee, they were still active in the U.N.I.A. But by this time the Garvey movement, which had thousands of followers in the New York and Philadelphia areas, was in trouble.

Garvey was suggesting that African-Americans turn to Africa as their spiritual home, but many black people did not want to associate themselves in any way with Africa. They complained to the government about Garvey. In addition to these people, the Bureau of Investigation under J. Edgar Hoover—later the F.B.I.—was also investigating Garvey. The Bureau considered anyone attempting to unite blacks as a possible threat to the security of the United States.

Garvey had been raising money for his various economic projects through the sales of stock, but he did not have the business experience needed for such a large operation. He formed a company and sold stock through the mail, but when his company's records were examined and found to be faulty, he was arrested and tried for mail fraud. Many people felt that Garvey had not been given a fair trial, but he was still found guilty and sent to a federal prison in Atlanta.

Earl Little sent several letters pleading for clemency for Garvey; one was intercepted by Bureau director J. Edgar Hoover.

The twenties in the East was a relatively good time for blacks. Black authors like Claude McKay and Langston Hughes were creating important works depicting the lives of their people. But in the Midwest, African-Americans were struggling, trying to find steady work, often moving from town to town to find it. By 1927 the Littles had moved from Milwaukee to Albion, Michigan.

During the period of African-American enslavement, Albion had been one of the "stations" on the Underground Railroad, the system of escape routes along which blacks

RESPECTFULLY REFERRED
FOR CONSIDERATION.

THE WHITE HOUSE
JUN 1 1927

1015 Galena Street,
Milwaukee, Wis.,
June 8th, 1927.

Hon. Calvin Coolidge,
The White House,
Washington, D.C.

JUN 13 1927
DEPT. OF JUSTICE

Honorable Sir:

We the officers and members of the International Industrial Club of Milwaukee, Wisconsin, and County of Milwaukee, do send you the following petition in behalf of Marcus Garvey, founder and President of the Universal Negro Improvement Association, who is now confined in the penitentiary at Atlanta, Georgia.

We now humbly petition your excellency in the Name of the God who created all men to dwell upon the face of the earth, to consider our request, that by the power vested in you, you release Marcus Garvey from the five-year sentence withour deportation which shall be your priceless gift to the Negro people of the world thus causing your name to be honored with generations yet unborn.

Your petitioners in duty ever pray.

L. Little, President

W.M. Townsend, Secretary

Robert Finney, Treasurer

Malcolm's father, Earl Little, sent letters requesting clemency for Marcus Garvey to several federal officials, including the President, Calvin Coolidge.

fled from southern plantations northward toward Canada. Immediately following the Civil War and the passage of the Thirteenth Amendment, which freed the enslaved Africans, many blacks lived with white citizens in Albion as housekeepers or servants.

Malcolm was barely four when the Little family moved into a farmhouse on the outskirts of Lansing, Michigan. But the new home would not be permanent for the still-growing family. Whites who were opposed to having black neighbors went to court and sued to reverse the sale of the house to the minister's family. The sale was illegal, they argued, because of a clause in the deed that said the land ". . . shall never be rented, leased, sold to, or occupied . . . by persons other than those of the Caucasian race."

Earl Little vowed to fight for the right to stay in the house he had bought. Two weeks after he made his brave decision the house was burned down. The fire was set in the middle of the night while the family slept. Elder Little thought that the fire must have been set by the people who didn't want a black family to live among them. The local fire department came, but did nothing to put out the fire. Malcolm and his brothers and sisters stood outside the house on the cold November night while the house burned to the ground.

The family moved to a house in East Lansing, Michigan, and were stoned by their white neighbors. East Lansing, a college town, had no low-income housing or "colored" neighborhood. Earl Little, fearing for the safety of his family, moved again, this time to the outskirts of town. The year was 1929, the beginning of the Great Depression.

Three of Malcolm's siblings (left to right): Wesley, Yvonne, and Reginald, in front of the Littles' home in Lansing, Michigan

By 1931 there were seven children in the Little family. Wilfred was the eldest child, then Hilda, followed by Philbert and Malcolm. Reginald, Yvonne, and Wesley were born after Malcolm. Elder Little continued to spread the word about the Garvey movement. He went from town to town, talking about the problems of black people and even became the head of a U.N.I.A. chapter in Indiana Harbor, Indiana.

Earl Little had taken Malcolm to U.N.I.A. meetings, had let him hear the rallying cry of its members to "Uplift the Race!" Malcolm had seen his father active in the meetings, had seen him speak to crowds of cheering African-Americans, and had seen the respect that he had both as the president of the Omaha branch of the U.N.I.A. and as an outstanding spiritual leader. And, although he most likely did not understand them all, Malcolm had also heard of the issues that faced black America.

By the time he was six, he had seen his father speak up time and time again for black people, and had seen his mother work with his father in the U.N.I.A. He had heard his father speak time and time again about Marcus Garvey and the need for all people of color to unite. Elder Little was the source of strength within his family and within the black communities where he traveled.

Then, on the twenty-eighth of September, 1931, Malcolm was again awakened in the middle of the night. This time it was not the house on fire, or angry neighbors trying to force the family to move. His mother was screaming. There were police in the living room, trying to calm her down. They took the tearful woman to Sparrow Hospital, where Earl Little lay dead.

Earl Little's crushed body had been found lying near a trolley track that ran between Lansing and East Lansing. The conductor of the trolley claimed not to have seen the huge black man and stated that somehow he must have approached the trolley on his own, then somehow fallen beneath its wheels. Louise Little believed her husband had

MAN RUN OVER BY STREET CAR

Earl Little, 41, Fatally Hurt; Thought to Have Fallen Under Truck

CORONER PLANS INQUEST

Believe Negro Lost Life Because He Forgot Coat, Left Earlier Car

Earl Little, 41, living at Jolly Corners, sustained fatal injuries late Monday night when he was run over by a street car at Detroit street and East Michigan avenue, a block east of the city limits.

The car was operated by William Hart, 1417 Vine street, who told Coroner Ray Gorsline that he did not see the man before the accident. It is believed that he fell under the rear trucks as he was running for the car.

Coroner Gorsline found that Little had taken another car which passed about 12 minutes before the car operated by Hart. He reached for his pocket when he boarded it, but told the motorman to let him off at the next corner. He did not have an overcoat on at this time, it was said, but did have an overcoat on when the accident occurred.

Went Back for Coat

It is believed that he discovered that he had forgotten his coat when he reached for his purse, and that he got off the car to go back for it. The coroner has been unable to discover where he left the coat. When he was found his purse and a street car check were in the overcoat pocket.

Coroner Gorsline planned to summon a coroner's jury for an inquest and expected to take the members of the jury to the scene of the accident Tuesday forenoon.

Little, a negro, leaves a widow, Mrs. Louise Little, 10 children, the parents, Mr. and Mrs. John Little of Reynolds, Ga., three sisters, and a brother, James Little of Albion. Funeral services will be held at the Buck Funeral home Thursday afternoon at 2 o'clock. The body will be taken to Georgia for interment.

A newspaper account of Earl Little's death

been killed by whites who did not want him to continue preaching the philosophy of Marcus Garvey. The police report said that the death would be investigated.

For any child it is difficult to believe that a father who was so central to his life could be so quickly taken away. Malcolm would never forget the night that his father was killed. He would remember the screams of his mother, and of the suddenly fatherless family huddled together in yet another tragedy.

Earl Little was dead, but he had left an impression on many African-Americans in Nebraska, Michigan, Wisconsin, and Indiana, places where he had taught and served black people. He had left an impression on these people and on the young, frightened person of Malcolm Little, his son.

2

The Son

WHEN Malcolm's father was killed in 1931, the country was in the middle of a depression. Every morning in the cities there were long lines of men and women looking for jobs, and sometimes just a meal to get them through the day. Nighttime found many of these same people sleeping under bridges and in old shacks on the edges of towns. Whites and blacks alike suffered as factories closed and steady employment was hard to find. For the Little family it was a time of near desperation.

With the death of his father, Malcolm felt insecure. The very idea that someone so close to him, someone he had considered so large and invincible, could suddenly be dead, was a shock. Malcolm hadn't had the chance to see his father before he died; Earl Little had not been there to reassure him the way he always had in the past. Nights were suddenly filled with the possibilities of terror and of sudden death. The six-year-old was afraid to go to sleep in the dark.

There had been another change in Malcolm's life. He had recently started school. Nearly all of the children who went to Pleasant Grove Elementary were white. Malcolm didn't mind that as long as they were nice, and most of them were. He knew that he couldn't stay home with his mother anymore. Most of the time she was out working, or looking for work.

Most black women in and around the Lansing and East Lansing areas did "day's work." They cleaned people's homes and were paid for the day's work. Local help-wanted ads offered white women five dollars a week for six or seven days' housekeeping. Black women made less. An eight-to-ten-hour workday would often bring Louise Little only fifty cents.

While Louise worked, Hilda took care of the younger children. There was no money for clothing. Malcolm had to wear what was handed down by his older brothers, and he was often teased about his poor clothing. Some of the white children in the school were also poor, but few as poor as the Littles.

Louise Little was an intelligent, well-educated woman who, had she been white, could have done better. She was

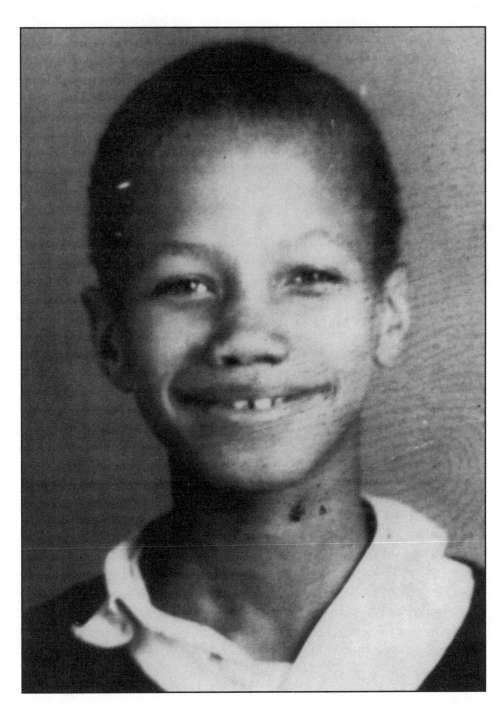

Malcolm Little during his school years

a proud woman, too. It was painful for her not to be able to take better care of her family. When she couldn't find work, or lost a job that she so desperately needed, Malcolm would see her crying. He would watch her try to hide the tears from the children.

Sometimes the family had barely enough to eat and would have to make soup out of wild dandelion greens they could gather. Malcolm would sometimes take the leftover greens to school the next day to eat for his lunch. Sometimes they only had cornmeal to eat, and their mother would make bread and soak it in whatever broth she could make.

There were times when Malcolm went to school without eating anything. Being very hungry gives you a sense of dizziness, as if you're going to pass out at any moment, and sometimes Malcolm would sit in class and hope that he wouldn't fall.

When he was nine or so, Malcolm and his brother Philbert would go out rabbit hunting. When they killed a rabbit, they would sell it to one of their white neighbors. Years later, Malcolm would understand that the neighbors would buy the rabbits just to help the Little family. Malcolm's family did not eat pork or rabbit meat, since both animals were considered "unclean" by many black families.

Malcolm's mother had to apply for help for the family, and they began to receive a small welfare check. Louise could not feed the children by herself, but for a long time she had resisted asking for help. When social workers visited the Little home they were surprised. Louise Little did not speak or act the way other blacks in the area did.

Malcolm's fourth-grade class at Pleasant Grove Elementary School

She spoke as an educated person, her early training in Grenada giving her already precise English a slightly British accent. She instructed her children that they were to be polite, but they did not have to either beg for assistance or feel that they had to be particularly grateful to the social workers. The few clothes and food supplies that Louise Little accepted she considered a loan, one that would have to be repaid. Louise did not like the way the people from the welfare office walked around her house, treating her family as if their feelings didn't matter. Malcolm began to notice how much the people from the welfare office bothered his mother and he began to resent them as well.

In Michigan, as in almost every state during the Depression, there were locations where, once or twice a month, free food was given to the needy. Only the poorest families were entitled to this food, and soon the Littles were among them. Children who saw Malcolm and his family at the food station said things to him in school, things that were very painful to him. But there was nothing he could do about it.

Not all of the children in school, or in the neighborhood where they lived, were mean to him. Many of them knew what it was like to be poor, and many were friendly to the Little children. Malcolm played with his white friends as well as with the blacks who lived nearby.

But something else was going on in Malcolm's house. The strain on his mother was beginning to show. Malcolm got into trouble. He had been caught stealing and one of the neighbors told the welfare investigator. The welfare investigator questioned his mother and, much to Malcolm's surprise, the usually strong woman began to cry. She said she could raise her own children, that she didn't need their help. She seemed more upset than Malcolm had ever seen her before. Malcolm had done something wrong, he had stolen, and he was ready to take whatever punishment was given to him, but he wasn't ready for his mother's odd behavior.

Louise Little began to sit for long periods of time without speaking. She acted as if she had suddenly forgotten to do those things she had always done around the house. She began to talk to nobody in particular, ignoring the questions of the children. Sometimes she would cry softly to herself for no apparent reason. Malcolm didn't like seeing his mother like that. He wanted to keep people away from her, to make the investigators stop asking her questions or asking him and his brothers and sisters questions about her. The children tried to take over the running of the house, to protect their mother, but things were getting difficult.

In school Malcolm could handle his assignments easily, but did not work as hard as his teachers thought he should have. Malcolm realized that he was bright. He was fairly popular, too. He could play sports and made his school basketball team. He enjoyed playing baseball and football with his schoolmates. In 1937 blacks were not allowed on most professional sports teams, but they were nevertheless making great strides in that direction. Joe Louis had become heavyweight champion of the world by knocking out James J. Braddock. It was about this time that Malcolm decided to try his hand at boxing. It was a disaster. It didn't take Malcolm long to discover that he wasn't going to be a "tough" guy. At any rate, he wasn't going to be tough *physically*. Mental toughness was another thing.

But while Joe Louis, from nearby Detroit, was becoming heavyweight champion of the world, other black people were still being lynched, or driven from their homes. In some places blacks who tried to vote lost their jobs. In some states blacks were arrested on minor charges with the intention of making them work on plantations, picking cotton or peanuts, when cheap labor was needed.

What the lynchings were all about, what the beatings and terrorizing were all about, was to force black people to remain second-class citizens. If you were an African-American there were things you were supposed to do, and things you were not supposed to do. Depending on where you lived in the United States, you were not supposed to vote, or to expect equal pay with whites, or live in white

**Joe Louis became heavyweight champion
of the world in 1937.**

neighborhoods. You were not supposed to take any right that whites had not given you. One of the things that African-American males were not supposed to do was to be too friendly to white females. All black males knew this. It was something that was told to you when you were a child. Stories of young black men being hung from trees or burned alive because they had associated with white women were told in every black home.

This constant threat to black America greatly affected how Malcolm reacted to his classmates. As Malcolm reached his early teen years, the years in which many young people start dating, or at least begin flirtations with classmates, Malcolm found himself in a school situation in which all of the girls were white.

In September, 1938, Malcolm was thirteen years old. He was tall, thin, with a wide smile and reddish hair that he wore short. He started the seventh grade and immediately began to have trouble in school. He had a series of conflicts with his teachers about his clowning around in class. The role of clown was probably what he felt, as if he were an actor trapped in a strange role in which he could never be himself. He couldn't tell people what was going on in his home, how his mother was talking to herself, how she seemed not to notice sometimes that the children were even there.

His mother's condition worsened. More and more she appeared to need help, but the only thing the state investigators seemed to be concerned with was proving that Louise was an unfit mother. It was frightening for Malcolm to see her drift away from the family. He had already lost his father, and now he knew he was losing his mother.

Investigators from the state of Michigan made plans to take Malcolm away from his family and put him into a home.

Malcolm was placed in the home of a black family, the Gohannas. While living with the Gohannas, he had enough to eat, but was saddened by the fact that he had been separated from his own family.

Malcolm was transferred from the Pleasant Grove school to West Junior High School.

Social workers continued to go to the Little house and to question the other children closely about their mother's behavior. Was she a good mother? How did she spend her time? Malcolm felt that the social workers were tearing apart the family unity. Louise Little had been through an extremely difficult time. She had had a good education, which she could not use because she was black. She had a philosophy of self-determination, which she could not exercise. She had pride in her race and her family, and that pride was being threatened as well. In January, 1939, she was declared legally insane and committed to a mental institution in Kalamazoo, Michigan. State social workers decided to place the younger children in foster homes, an event that would always be a source of bitterness for Malcolm. Wilfred and Hilda were allowed to live in the house the Littles had called home for so many years.

By the age of thirteen, Malcolm had seen his house burn down. He had been exposed to the violent death of his father, had known extreme hunger, had seen the slow breakdown of his mother, and had also seen brothers and sisters placed in homes.

He began to have troubles at West Junior High. On one

occasion he put a thumbtack on a teacher's chair. He wasn't surprised when he was expelled from the school. He thought he simply would not go to school anymore, but found instead that he was being made a ward of the state, and being sent to reform school.

He was transferred to a county juvenile home in Mason,

Malcolm Little was sent to a county juvenile home in Mason, Michigan.

Michigan, some twelve miles from Lansing. The Swerleins, a family hired to run the group home in Mason, were friendly to Malcolm. They saw nothing wrong, however, in referring to Malcolm and other blacks as "niggers."

Malcolm got along well with the Swerleins. He tried hard to please them, and they seemed to like him. He was supposed to be transferred to the reform school, but instead he was enrolled in the junior high school at Mason. He was the only black student in the eighth grade, but ranked as the best student in most subjects. In his second semester he was elected class president.

Sometimes he was hassled in school by white boys who were tougher than he was. While Malcolm was still upset about the breakup of his family, and his mother's being placed in an institution, he was trying as hard as he could to get along with the students in Mason. Malcolm states, in his autobiography, that during this time he tried to be as "white" as possible.

Again he was caught in a conflict. By acting in a "white" way he was doing well. But he wasn't white, and he couldn't act as if he were, because he was still being called a nigger by kids who didn't like him, and he knew there were things he could and couldn't do because he was black.

During this period he became quieter, staying more to himself than he had earlier on. Malcolm was facing what all teenagers face: that moment in time when he had to look beyond what was happening from day to day and decide what he wanted to do in the future.

He understood that he was bright. His grades at Mason

The Roxbury section of Boston, Massachusetts

proved as much. He knew how he ranked when compared to some of his classmates. He heard their plans for high school, college, and beyond. Some wanted to be doctors; others thought about opening stores, or going into law enforcement.

Malcolm played basketball for the school team. When he played at other schools, some of the kids in the stands would call him racial names. The schools sometimes held dances after the basketball games. Malcolm would go to the dances, but knew he wasn't supposed to dance with the white girls that attended them, and there were rarely any black girls.

It was during this period of Malcolm's life that he met Ella, his half sister. Earl Little had been married previously and had had three children. One daughter was grown now and lived in Boston. She invited Malcolm to Boston, and he took the long trip by Greyhound bus to see her. He wore his best suit and carried some spare underwear and shirts in a cardboard suitcase. Malcolm had never been to a big city before, and he was fascinated by the pace, the music, and the fast life of Boston.

When he returned to Mason he was full of stories about his trip, and full of wonder about what it would be like to live in a place like Boston.

Malcolm continued to do well at Mason Junior High. He was, in fact, doing what he was supposed to do to be part of American society. He was studying and working hard to succeed by doing the right thing. One day at school, one of Malcolm's teachers asked him what he wanted to do with his life. The teacher was one of Malcolm's favorites. He had always done well in his classes and thought the teacher liked him.

Malcolm hadn't thought much about what he wanted to be when he finished school, but he told the teacher that he wanted to be a lawyer. He had expected the teacher to be pleased with his choice since he had always encouraged his pupils, trying to get them to push themselves, to explore their limits.

But instead of being pleased with Malcolm's choice of profession, the teacher seemed upset. He reassured Malcolm that he liked him, but then told him that he had to be realistic.

> *We all here like you, you know that. But you've got to be realistic about being a nigger. A lawyer — that's no realistic goal for a nigger. You need to think about something you can be. You're good with your hands. Why don't you plan on carpentry?*
>
> —The Autobiography of Malcolm X

This encounter with his teacher was a turning point in Malcolm's life. It was not a shock that the teacher would discourage him from being a lawyer. Malcolm knew that he was black and that blacks were not expected to succeed. He also knew that few blacks in Michigan went on to high school. There were few law schools in the country that even accepted black students. But Malcolm, like so many young black men, had thought that doing the right thing, being smart, and getting good marks,

Malcolm at fourteen

would work for him even though he was black.

The teacher probably thought he was doing Malcolm a favor by preparing him for what life was going to offer him as a black person. Malcolm's classmates tried to cheer him up, but it wasn't helpful. On that day Malcolm, in many ways, simply gave up on the American dream.

Again Malcolm began to withdraw. As his classmates began to plan for their graduation, and to talk about courses they would take in high school, Malcolm would avoid them. Very few blacks had ever gone to high school in Mason. They weren't expected to go beyond the eighth grade. And why should they, when they wouldn't be hired for most jobs that required more education?

Malcolm was still corresponding with Ella. She invited him to come live with her in Boston.

To Malcolm the city of Boston was a completely different world. Where Mason, Lansing, and East Lansing had been considerably smaller in population than Boston, they were light-years behind in sophistication. What's more, Boston had an old established black population and a history of civil rights.

It was in Boston that two of the most famous fugitive slave cases, that of Anthony Burns and later of George Latimer, had been tried. Burns had been returned to the South, but Latimer's freedom had been purchased by local blacks. And, during the Civil War, it was from Boston that the famous 54th Massachusetts Volunteers, the black regiment that stormed the walls at Fort Wagner, sailed.

Malcolm had never seen blacks so well dressed, so relaxed in the streets, or so fully participating in the life of the city, as in Boston.

Ella was family. She was prepared to help Malcolm make the adjustments necessary to live in a big city. Malcolm, with nothing left for him in Mason, accepted her invitation.

Malcolm spent days just making himself familiar with the streets of Boston. He loved Roxbury, the black section, and the exciting life that was offered there. He also found the museums and the libraries that dotted the city.

Ella warned the youngster to try to find friends of high caliber. The friends that Malcolm found, however, were not of the "high class" that Ella had hoped for. He came upon a pool hall in which he saw young black men relaxing, kidding each other, and shooting pool. The young men were "sharp" dressers and used a lot of street talk. Malcolm watched them for a while from outside the pool hall, and then ventured inside.

"Shorty" was a young man whom Malcolm met at the pool hall. He knew his way around Boston, and was open with Malcolm. But most of all, he hinted of ways that a black man could make it in the streets of Boston without finishing high school.

What Malcolm needed was a way of finding value in his own life, of building up the self-esteem that had been so damaged in Michigan. From his parents he had received training as a young boy that intelligence was valuable to the black race, and could be used, along with hard work, to succeed. But after the death of his father this seemed to all slip away. His intelligence was not appreciated and was finally dismissed by a teacher who urged him to understand how blacks were limited. There was no doubt that what Shorty was doing was a lot less than Malcolm's father had expected of Malcolm, but Shorty wasn't walking around with his head down or feeling bad about himself. When Shorty talked, telling him how blacks could make it in Boston, Malcolm listened, and listened carefully.

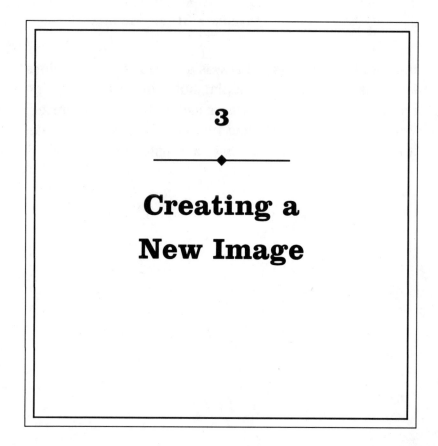

3

Creating a
New Image

SHORTY was from Lansing, Michigan. That made Malcolm his "homeboy." He liked Malcolm and decided to teach him the ropes. He also got him a job as a shoeshine boy in the Roseland State Ballroom.

Style. It was about style. The shoeshine rags and brushes were to go by one footrest; the polish bottles, paste wax, and suede brushes were all to be within reach so that the shine would go smoothly. Customers liked to have a shoeshine boy who looked as if he knew what he was doing, as if he belonged to the job.

Malcolm was to watch the urinals, as well. When a man finished using one and washed his hands, Malcolm would hurry over with a towel, hoping for a tip.

" . . . Tom a little — white cats especially like that . . ." Freddie, the old shoeshine boy, had hit the number and bought a Cadillac. Now he was showing Malcolm the work.

Roseland itself was an exciting place. The big bands played there, including Duke Ellington's, and Count Basie's. The music was the best that Malcolm had ever heard.

**One of the big bands that played
at Roseland State Ballroom was Duke Ellington's.**

The sounds of all of the records he had heard back in Lansing now filtered through the bathroom doors.

Malcolm learned how to shine shoes, how to make the rag pop in rhythm, and how to put on a show for the customer. Brushing off a customer's coat as he looked into the bathroom mirror, a broad smile when accepting a quarter tip, were all part of the game. Hustle up the tips, make money in the role of shoeshine boy/flunky boy/towel boy/smiling boy, and then step back from the role to live the way they wanted to live in Roxbury.

Roxbury. Ella lived in the Hill area, the more stable area of the black community. She didn't like Malcolm shining shoes, and she didn't like him spending his time in lower Roxbury. But Malcolm liked the more exciting area, with its pool halls and dives. In its streets he saw blacks who laughed easily among themselves, who had their own set of values, and who gave each other value and respect in ways that did not depend on the white world.

What held them together, at least on the surface, was style. They looked and dressed a certain way, they played cards, smoked "reefer," and shot craps. Whether you won or lost at craps wasn't that important. If you won you bought the beers at the party; if you lost you still went to the party, but had to wait until a friend bought you the beers.

Malcolm began to talk like the other young men who frequented the pool hall. In Roxbury you could tell who a person was by the way he or she spoke. Did they use the latest slang? Did they know enough to call a white person an "ofay"? Did they know what "going through changes" meant? And the sure way of being rejected was to be a "square," someone who did not know what was happening on the streets of Roxbury. The blacks on the Hill might have rejected the people in Roxbury, but the stylish down-to-earth people in Roxbury were also rejecting the so-called "elites" of Boston.

Malcolm learned the language of inner-city Roxbury easily, and learned something else. In Roxbury, your intelligence and know-how were measured in different ways than they were in the other places in which he had lived. In Lansing your survival was dependent on the goodwill of white folks, and what you knew didn't matter much if you were black. In Roxbury what you knew was the only thing that was going to get you over. And what you had to know was how to deal with people, how to survive in the streets, and how to hustle up a dollar and an image.

The first thing that Malcolm needed for his new image was a zoot suit. The zoot suit might have been the wildest outfit that any American wore since powdered wigs, and Malcolm's was as wild as any. He found that he could buy a zoot suit on credit and went immediately to a local clothing store.

Malcolm's suit was sky-blue, with the high waist fitting fairly snugly. The legs of the suit flared out to thirty inches at the knee and then were sharply tapered to only twelve inches at the ankle. Malcolm had to take his shoes off and point his toes to get his foot through the narrow opening.

The jacket of the zoot suit had exaggerated padded shoulders and tapered down to the waist before flaring out inches above the knee. He bought a matching sky-blue hat with a super broad brim and a blue feather on the side. The store owner gave him the final required accessory for the zoot suit: the long gold chain that hung from the belt, looped down below the coat and up into the pocket. Malcolm was sharp!

He had pictures taken of himself and was pleased with his new image, except for his hair.

Malcolm had worn his hair short in Michigan; now he let it grow long enough to have it "conked." The word *conk* came from congolene, a caustic substance used in the forties and fifties which, when put on the naturally curly hair of blacks, flattened it out. It was done in black barbershops across the country, but many young people did it, or tried to do it, for themselves.

Shorty helped Malcolm get the chemicals to make the conk. A can of lye, white potatoes, and eggs made up the basic mixture.

Malcolm watched as Shorty sliced the potatoes as thin as he could and put them into a Mason jar. Then he poured in the lye, which reacted with the potatoes. The potatoes diluted the lye. The result was a jelly-like mixture. Shorty added the eggs, which would make the homemade conk stick longer to the hair.

Shorty put an apron around Malcolm, fastening it tightly around the neck. He told Malcolm to feel the jar. Malcolm put his hand around the jar. It was hot.

" . . . That's the lye," Shorty said. "So you know it's going to burn when I comb it in. It's going to burn bad."

Next Shorty combed out Malcolm's hair, using Vaseline. Then he put as much of the Vaseline as he could on Malcolm's skin around the hairline and on his ears. He didn't want the lye to touch Malcolm's skin if he could help it.

Shorty used a metal straightening comb to apply the lye mixture to Malcolm's hair. Malcolm could only think of one thing — Shorty was right, it burned!

A good conk went as close to the scalp as possible, and burned like crazy. Malcolm gritted his teeth as Shorty worked as quickly and as carefully as he could. When he finished, he washed the area around Malcolm's neck, and wiped away any lye that ran from his hair. Malcolm looked in the mirror. His long red hair was as flat and shiny as any white man's. He had his first conk.

The zoot suit and the conk had a special significance for young blacks from Roxbury to Harlem to the inner cities across the country. They were the styles of choice for these young men, the styles that made them distinctive from the "squares" of the world. But there was also another significance. The only reason these young men could wear these outfits that many people felt were, at best, strange, was because they were being excluded from the jobs that demanded more conventional dress. Banks would never allow their employees to dress in zoot suits, and neither would the big insurance companies in downtown Boston. But Shorty and Malcolm and the young black men in Roxbury knew they would never be hired by these companies anyway. If they weren't going to be allowed into conventional society, then they might as well be sharp. And there was nothing as sharp as a zoot suit.

Malcolm learned how to dress, how to hustle tips at Roseland, how to talk "hip," and how to dance. Malcolm needed a way to feel good about himself. If being a lawyer was not "practical" for a black man, then Malcolm would look somewhere else for personal value. He was finding it in the style and energy of Roxbury.

Malcolm Little, in Boston, was not the same person as the Malcolm Little who had been in Lansing, or in Mason. Part of the American dream is the hope that one day the dreamer will share in the adventure and excitement that defines what this country is all about. The dreamer hopes both to make a contribution and to benefit from participation in American society. While Malcolm was in Lansing and in Mason he still thought, like so many other youngsters of his age, that he would one day take his place in American society. By the time he had immersed himself in the culture and life-styles of Roxbury, he no longer shared that dream. Now he was a young man resigned to the idea that the color of his skin would keep him forever on the outside of American society.

Malcolm found that blacks were not the only ones excluded from American society. There were whites who frequented the same Roxbury bars and pool halls as the blacks. Malcolm had several girlfriends and one of them, a girl named Sophia, was white.

At this time Malcolm was living a life that was not involved with race. Like most teenagers, he was thinking primarily of his own clothing, and his own pleasures.

December, 1941. The U.S. entered World War II. Malcolm had worked as a shoeshine boy, as a clerk in a drugstore, and as a busboy in a restaurant. He was sixteen. The Depression was still affecting the economy, especially for

**One of Malcolm's jobs as a teen was as
a sandwich seller on the railroad.**

black men. Many black men did not have steady employment, and many would never rise above the position of
laborer. For a teenager, jobs were few and far between.

A friend of Ella's got Malcolm a job on the railroad as
a kitchen helper. Being a kitchen helper meant that he
would be washing dishes, cleaning up after the regular
cooks, bagging and disposing of garbage, and washing
down the stoves and counters in the rolling kitchen. It
was considered an excellent job for a black man. Malcolm
worked first at the train yard, loading food onto the trains
and doing general chores around the Dover Street Yard.
Early in 1942 he got his first chance to travel when he
was assigned to the New York to Boston run. He washed

tons of dirty dishes and silverware as an efficient kitchen crew prepared meals around him. The black railroad cooks and Pullman car porters were among the most respected workers in black America. Malcolm was surprised to find that many of the men who worked the railroads had college degrees.

Malcolm worked in the kitchen for months before the opportunity came for him to work as a sandwich man. As a sandwich man he found himself selling ham-and-cheese sandwiches and coffee cake on the speeding train, lugging the heavy five-gallon jug of coffee through the rocking cars, and trying to smile at potential customers as he struggled to keep his balance. It was during this time that he first visited Washington, D.C., and Harlem.

Some black people talk about how they felt upon reaching Africa for the first time. It is not simply ancestral roots that made them feel at home, but that for the first time in their lives they were in the majority. It was the black race that dominated the streets, that looked at them over the counters of stores, and of banks, that wore the uniforms of the police and of the postmen. It is often expressed that Africa gives American blacks a sense of relief from a tension that they never fully understood they suffered from. This is the same relief that many people feel when they first visit New York City's Harlem. Malcolm Little arrived in Harlem in his late teens. He, too, was home.

One of the interesting features of Harlem, before the period of integration, was that the community had an outstanding mix of people. Black judges lived in Harlem because they couldn't live in many places outside of the vibrant black community. Wealthy black doctors lived in Harlem in the forties because they weren't allowed to move into white affluent neighborhoods, even though they could afford to do so. It was not unusual for prominent novelists, poets, and composers to have an afternoon drink in Small's Paradise, a favorite Harlem bar, sitting next to politicians and postal clerks.

Harlem was exciting, and tough. Many blacks were finding jobs because of World War II, and the nightlife was picking up. Malcolm saw the excitement of the nightlife, and he saw the poverty that was much of Harlem.

Malcolm got a job at Small's and began to learn from some of the men who ran the rackets in Harlem just what was going on in Harlem's underworld. He saw that the men engaged in such businesses as the "numbers" game, an illegal lottery based on horse racing, were as well respected as people who held steady jobs. The men who controlled the various hustles were always looking for bright young men, and Malcolm was obviously bright. They offered him the opportunity to make money working for them, and he accepted their offer.

When Malcolm had moved to Boston to live with Ella he had entered a new phase of his life. For the first time he had choices to make about how he would live. The choices he made were the ones he saw available for a young black man.

Malcolm could have continued his education in Boston if he had had both a strong desire to go to high school and a belief that more school would have benefited him. But he had already been discouraged from continuing his

education. What was more, he had seen black men with
college educations working on the same jobs that he had
worked.

What Malcolm wanted to do, more than anything else,

**Small's Paradise, a hangout for artists, politicians,
poets, and hustlers in Harlem**

was to bring value to his life. He wanted to be looked upon as a person who had the respect of his fellow human beings. By the time he reached Harlem he was convinced that the respect he wanted would only be found within the black community.

4

Detroit Red

O N the seventh of December, 1941, the Japanese Army
had attacked Pearl Harbor, bringing the United States
firmly into the Second World War. African-Americans had
fought in every war the United States had been in. Black
patriots had fought in the Revolutionary War, had manned
ships in the War of 1812, had fought for the Union in the
Civil War, had fought under Teddy Roosevelt in the
Spanish-American War and in the trenches of Europe during
the First World War. Despite these facts, the armed forces

were still segregated. Black soldiers served in all-black units, usually under white officers. Black American fliers at Tuskegee Institute in Alabama were still trying to win the right to help defend their country. Most blacks who were accepted in the armed forces during the Second World War were employed as laborers or service workers.

But even while some black Americans were serving their country, the bulk of black Americans in the States were still living as second-class citizens. In Harlem the best a black person with a college degree could hope for was a job in a black organization or as a clerk in a black neighborhood store, unless he or she was fortunate enough to be a professional such as a teacher, a lawyer, or a doctor. Even then, for the most part, the choices were limited. A person without a degree had little chance of even working in the telephone company at the beginning of the war.

Malcolm was eighteen years old in 1943 and, like many young black men his age, drifted from job to job. In between the jobs, he claims, in his autobiography, that he was a street hustler. He sold marijuana, gambled, and ran numbers for big-time mobsters. By this time he had been given the name of "Detroit Red" by his friends, and it was as "Detroit Red" that he viewed himself as a streetwise sharpie. Was Malcolm really as much of a street hustler and petty criminal as he says in his autobiography? During the war years Harlem was full of men who were older, more experienced, and a lot tougher than Malcolm Little.

But street hustling did serve black men in a very special way. When there were no jobs available outside of the community, illegal activities such as the numbers lottery were the only employment opportunities. Sometimes

Detroit Red

these jobs were the difference between men being self-supporting or being on welfare. What was more, in a social system that values intelligence more than brawn, the street hustle was the only way that black men could use their intelligence.

It was also true that many of the street hustles that Malcolm was involved in were not considered true crimes by the Harlem community. They were known to be crimes as far as the law was concerned, though, and Harlemites fully expected to be arrested if caught by the police. Many people felt that the laws were only directed against blacks anyway. In the Prohibition era blacks were arrested for making whiskey in basement stills. But when selling liquor was legalized, it was whites who owned the liquor stores.

Years later, when the numbers lottery was legalized, the black numbers dealers who had spent years paying off police and risking arrest were put out of business, and whites were put into the executive positions of the numbers lottery in New York City.

Malcolm knew that what he was doing was considered criminal activity and understood that in almost any illegal activity some people would be hurt. Nevertheless he continued his hustling until he ran into trouble with the organized mobs he dealt with.

Malcolm, during this period of his life, learned a great deal about life in Harlem. He learned the streets, the bars, the apartment houses that served as after-hours joints and those that were houses of prostitution. He learned about the storefront churches, the huge, established churches, and the men who led the congregations.

Most of all, he learned about the people of Harlem.

During his younger days in Lansing, when he had to watch the slow breaking up of his family, he had learned to be an observer. Now he learned to observe the people he dealt with. He knew what troubled them, and what pleased them. He knew what the men faced as they tried to hold their families together, and what daily humiliations they tried to drown in Harlem bars. He learned how desperately they clung to dreams of wealth, playing the numbers in hope of the one break that would help them to realize their ambitions. He knew how easily some of the younger men, men who knew how drugs destroyed lives, still became addicted. He used drugs himself, and he began to pull small holdups. He knew how many people had just turned off their minds, had given up on life and had, in a way, become spiritually dead. He himself had become spiritually dead.

When Malcolm ran into trouble with the New York gangs, he returned to the familiar haunts of Boston.

In 1945 the Second World War ended and the white males who had left their jobs and homes were returning. Factories that had made war goods were closing down, and the consumer boom had not yet begun. Blacks who had found employment during the war were suddenly laid off. Malcolm didn't even try looking for work. He decided to team up with Sophia, the white girl he had known, her sister, another girl, and two other black male friends, to pull off some house burglaries.

The girls would look over the house, decide when the owners would be out and how best to break in, then report their findings to Malcolm and the other men. For a while the burglaries were successful.

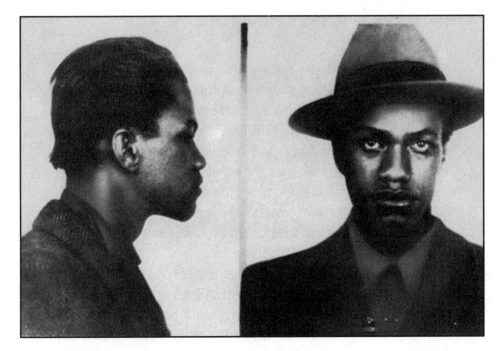

Malcolm's mug shot

Then Malcolm made a mistake. He took a stolen watch to a shop to have the crystal repaired. The owner of the shop had been notified to look out for stolen jewelry, and a description of the jewelry, including the watch, had been given to him. When Malcolm returned to pick up the watch, the police were waiting for him.

The three girls who had been part of Malcolm's "gang" were rounded up and questioned. They were released on low bail. Malcolm and one of the men were given high bails and were kept locked up.

Malcolm confessed to his crimes. He had been caught with the stolen jewelry, and at the time of his arrest had a gun in his possession.

The trial was held during the last week of February, 1946. The three white girls sat at the defense table, while Malcolm and the man he was arrested with were kept in a locked cage. The girls testified that they were afraid of Malcolm, and that they had been forced to commit the crimes. Malcolm saw that he would be on trial as much for associating with the white girls as he would be for the burglary. Despite his confession, he at first pleaded not guilty, but during the trial changed his plea to guilty. The judge accepted the plea.

The sentence most observers expected for burglaries of the kind that Malcolm had committed was two to three years. He had been arrested previously on a minor charge and did not seem to be a hardened criminal. After the judge had given the girls very light sentences, he then pronounced sentence on Malcolm. It was eight to ten years of hard labor.

Malcolm was taken to the Charlestown State Prison, across the Charles River from Boston. At the prison he was photographed and fingerprinted. Prisoner Number 22843 was told in no uncertain terms what kind of behavior was expected of him while he was in the ancient prison.

There was no running water in the small cell. Each prisoner was given what was called a slop bucket to use. He would urinate and defecate in the bucket and empty it when it was his turn to do so each day. If the stench became unbearable, or the flies nearly too much to take, it was unfortunate. There was no dining room; each inmate ate in his cell. Life would not be easy.

Malcolm had entered a new phase of his life. Two things were going to happen to him over the following years. The

Charlestown State Prison

first was that he would grow older, and with his aging there would be a certain maturing. The second thing would be that he would have a lot of time to think about his life, and about what he would do with that life.

What makes a person human is not simply that he or she is born with a certain form, but that he or she has strengths and weaknesses that make each human both interesting and different from his or her fellow humans. But prisons strive to remove these differences. Instead of having individual names, prisoners are assigned numbers, are made to rise in the morning at the same time, and to eat at the same time, and to act as much like one another as possible. Any major deviation from this is usually punished.

The twenty-year-old Malcolm was put into prison with people who had stolen, who had killed, who were career criminals. To escape this dehumanizing process, to remain an alert, vital person, Malcolm needed to separate himself from the bulk of the prison population. To do this he relied on the fact that he was bright. He began to read as much as he could and also began taking a correspondence course in English.

Malcolm had heard about an experimental prison reform plan in Massachusetts. The program was being conducted at an institution in Norfolk, Massachusetts.

The program at Norfolk provided the prisoners with considerably more freedom than was available at either Charlestown or Concord Reformatory. Malcolm appealed to the Massachusetts prison authorities on a number of occasions to transfer him there. Usually the program was considered good for those prisoners with the best chance of rehabilitation, and eventually Malcolm was accepted.

What the Norfolk institution offered primarily, besides the ability to individualize one's life, was an excellent library. Malcolm began to upgrade his reading. It was here that Malcolm learned about the great religions of the world, including that of Islam.

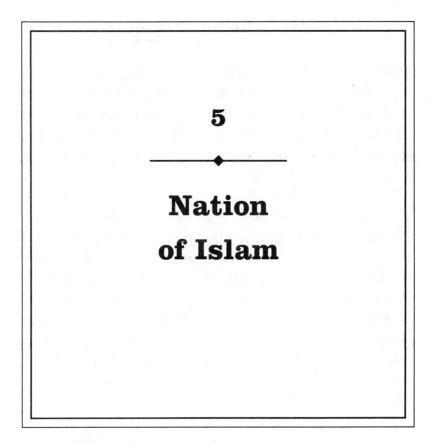

5

◆

Nation
of Islam

S HORTLY AFTER Malcolm went to prison, he received a
letter from his brother Philbert. The letter was one of
sympathy, saying that the members of Philbert's church
would pray for Malcolm. Malcolm, who had been raised
in a religious household, and whose father had been a
spiritual leader, had grown away from all religious feelings.
He wrote to his brother and told him that he did not want
his church's prayers.

Later, Malcolm received other letters from his family,

but the most influential one was from Reginald, who was a minister in something called the Nation of Islam. Reginald advised him to keep his body clean, and not to eat pork or smoke cigarettes. Malcolm soon discovered that several of his brothers and sisters had joined the Nation of Islam.

The Nation of Islam was both a political and religious movement that had been founded in the thirties as an answer to the urban misery that plagued blacks who lived in the cities across the United States. It was a nationalistic movement, one that would work for the creation of a black nation either outside of the United States or in some distinct part of the United States. It was also a separatist movement, in that its followers believed that people of color should separate themselves from white people.

The Nation of Islam was also a religious movement embracing the religion of Islam but, especially in its early days, there were important differences between their religious beliefs and those of the traditional followers of Islam in Africa, the Middle East, and Asia. One of the major differences was the importance of race in the Nation of Islam. Also, nearly all of the followers of the Nation of Islam in the United States were converts from other religions, and there were few religious teachers in this country to train them. But the lack of trained teachers did not stop new people from joining the group.

Reginald's letter suggested to Malcolm that the religion of Islam seemed a more natural religion for a black man than did Christianity. Malcolm had grown unsure about all religions. Life had not been good to him, and God had

Malcolm's brothers (left to right): Philbert, Wesley, Wilfred, and Reginald

not helped him. Still, he felt, almost instinctively, that he should listen to his brothers. The next time pork was served in the prison dining hall, he refused to eat it. He was surprised at the reaction of the fellow prisoners, especially the white prisoners. He liked setting himself apart from them, even if it was just a small thing such as not eating pork.

The problem with Christianity for many blacks was not the religious philosophy that it embraced, but the way it was presented in the United States.

Most Christians living in the United States had long lived with images of Jesus Christ that had been created by whites. In many black homes, pictures of a white, blue-eyed Jesus with long brown hair and vaguely Nordic features hung prominently in the living rooms. Not only did the pictures of Jesus not look like the black people who were worshiping Him, but He didn't even look as if He were from the area of Israel or the Middle East.

Moreover, much of the worship in Christianity has color images in which white is considered good, and black is considered bad, as in the spiritual "Open Your Heart":

If you don't believe you can be redeemed
Follow me down to the Jordan stream
He'll take your sins away, make you white as snow
Only the Holy Ghost can save your dying soul

Asians worshiped Asian-looking gods, Africans worshiped African-looking gods, and Europeans worshiped European-looking gods. Only African-Americans worshiped a god that looked like the people who had enslaved them! During the period in which African-Americans were enslaved, some white ministers had used the Bible to justify slavery.

Certainly the discovery of Islam was not new to African-Americans. Marcus Garvey, in his paper *Negro World*, had given a great deal of space to news about the Islamic world and had acknowledged that much of the African world was Islamic. The paper had even printed poetry in praise of Islam.

Reginald came to the prison and began to talk to Malcolm.

"You don't even know who you are," Reginald said. " . . . You don't know your true family name, you wouldn't recognize your true language if you heard it."

Malcolm listened as his brother spoke passionately about the Nation of Islam, and about how there were devils in the world. The devils were white people.

When Reginald left, Malcolm carefully considered what had been said. He thought about the whites in his own life: the judge who had sentenced him, the social workers who had called his mother crazy, the people who had so casually referred to African-Americans as "niggers."

Malcolm had turned away from religion in his teen years, had even ridiculed those people who turned to prayer to help them in their troubles. Now, in prison and more alone than he had ever been in his life, he was about to turn back, to revive himself from spiritual death.

The Nation of Islam, he had been told by prison inmates who had converted, was not just a religion. It was a movement mostly of African-Americans. It was headed by a man called the Honorable Elijah Muhammad. Philbert, Malcolm's brother, prompted him to write to Muhammad.

Malcolm wrote to Muhammad and patiently waited for an answer. In the meantime he continued his studies. But this time he was studying for himself, and not for the praise of a teacher. He took a correspondence course in Latin. He attended lectures offered by visiting scholars from Harvard and Yale. He read biographies of Hannibal, Ibn Saud, Marx, Lenin, Stalin, Hitler, Rommel, Gandhi, Patrick Henry, and John Brown.

He read H.G. Wells and Will Durant. He read volumes of

black history and the philosophy of Plato, Aristotle, Spinoza, Nietzsche, and Schopenhauer. He would not miss this chance for education.

The reply from the Honorable Elijah Muhammad came, along with some money, intended as a gift for the young prisoner.

What Elijah Muhammad said to Malcolm in the letter was not to consider himself a criminal. No man, in a just system, would resort to criminal activity, he said. You are not the criminal. The criminals are the whites who, through their racism, have forced you into the acts you have committed.

Malcolm felt that he had lived a bad life, that he had turned away from those values he considered worthwhile. He wanted to be a better human being, and the Nation of Islam was offering him that way.

"The very enormity of my previous life's guilt prepared me to accept the truth," he said in his autobiography.

Malcolm was not only ready to accept Islam as presented to him in prison, but he was willing to accept it with all of his heart, and without question.

6

The Message

THE Nation of Islam had its start in Detroit, Michigan, around the year 1930. A man who claimed to have been born in Mecca, the holy city of the Islamic people, began to teach among the black population at that time. At first the man, who called himself Wallace Fard Muhammad, merely taught the differences between the way the people in Detroit were living and the way the people in Saudi Arabia were living. Increasingly, though, he was discussing the relationships between whites and blacks.

The message that Wallace Fard Muhammad was delivering fell on ears eager to hear something that would relieve the condition of the blacks who lived in Detroit. He told his students, mostly poor people who had migrated from the South in search of jobs, that there were dietary laws they needed to follow, and that they needed to change the way they were living. They could not spend their time in useless entertainment, but had to become more serious in their approach to life.

There was a strong religious element in the teachings. Although Fard Muhammad taught from the familiar Christian Bible, he stated that it was not the right book to teach from. The right book, he said, was the *Qu'ran*, the holy book of the Islamic religion. He also established a house of worship in Detroit.

By following his teachings, Fard Muhammad claimed that the blacks of Detroit, many of whom were desperately poor, could overcome their white slave masters.

Fard Muhammad was a superior organizer. He created, within the temple in Detroit, the Muslim Girls Training Class, an academic school, and the Fruit of Islam, men trained for self-defense. Fard Muhammad allowed local ministers to run most of his programs. But just as Fard Muhammad had suddenly appeared on the Detroit scene in 1930, he left it just as suddenly four years later, in 1934. The man who took his place was born Elijah Poole, in Sandersville, Georgia, in 1896.

Poole settled in Detroit in 1923 and was, for a while, active in the Garvey movement. By 1930 the Garvey movement had lost much of its power and Poole, along with

Elijah Muhammad

two of his brothers, became active in the movement of
Fard Muhammad. It was under Fard Muhammad's leadership that Elijah Poole changed his name to Elijah Muhammad. When Fard Muhammad left the movement in
1934, it was Elijah Muhammad who continued the development of what by then had become known as the Nation
of Islam.

The Nation of Islam differed from most religious organizations in several ways. The first was that the beliefs

A gathering of Nation of Islam members

binding the members had more to do with race than with religion. To belong to the early Nation of Islam one had to be non-white. There were some Arab members, and a few Japanese members, but the overwhelming bulk of the membership was black. Whites were looked upon as the enemy of the non-white membership.

The Nation of Islam encouraged the membership of all black people, including the lowest economic group and those with the lowest community standing. Where Christianity demanded that one be free from sin, the Nation of Islam accepted those who were actively sinning and tried to reform them.

The Nation of Islam, both under Fard Muhammad and later under Elijah Muhammad, identified the major problems of African-Americans: that whites were constantly attacking blacks physically and psychologically. That whites wanted to maintain a social order in which blacks were in an inferior position and that they often did this by making blacks fearful of white violence. That whites also wanted to be financially superior to blacks and that they maintained their financial advantage by keeping blacks dependent on whites for income. That whites wanted to be able to manipulate blacks to their own advantage, and they worked to undermine black self-assurance so that they could do this. Then, finally, that blacks, ignorant of their own history, had developed a self-hatred that helped whites in their schemes.

To counter these massive attacks against blacks, the Nation of Islam devised a counterstrategy. The first thing that blacks had to do, they said, was to educate themselves. Self-knowledge of African life would prevent blacks from having feelings of inferiority, and knowledge of the world would allow them to fulfill their potential.

Basic to the Nation of Islam was the right to self-defense. They did not believe in being aggressive toward anyone, but insisted that no one could attack a black man, woman, or child without suffering the same kind of hostility.

Economic development of the black community was another major goal of the Nation of Islam. As long as blacks felt that they had to go to whites for jobs, or for money to buy houses or to invest in businesses, they would be under the economic control of the whites who had those jobs and the capital.

The first step, however, in the strategy of the Nation of Islam, was to free blacks from psychological dependence on whites. Elijah Muhammad, the head of the Nation of Islam, taught his followers that the white man was the enemy of the black man. Once the white man was accepted as the enemy, the separation of the races was made easy, as was a change in the behavior of the black man. Blacks who accepted Elijah Muhammad's teachings had only to ask themselves how would they live without going along with the desires of their enemies?

These beliefs were especially appealing to the kinds of people that the Nation of Islam attracted. But many African-Americans did not believe that the strategy would work. Basically they believed that only a few white Americans were against blacks, and that most blacks could enter the mainstream of American life by following the traditional paths.

The membership of the Nation of Islam consisted, in the early fifties, primarily of lower-class young men, loosely organized and largely ineffective outside of their own activities. Malcolm knew nothing of the group before being approached by his brothers.

But Malcolm started thinking about his own life and how, under different circumstances, he could have been the lawyer he had once told his teacher in Mason, Michigan, that he wanted to be. He wondered how many other black men, how many other prisoners in prisons across the country, could have and should have led useful, productive lives. People didn't want to be criminals.

Malcolm continued to study the teachings of Elijah Muhammad that were sent to him by his brothers. He also began debating other prisoners and teams from visiting colleges, including Harvard and Yale.

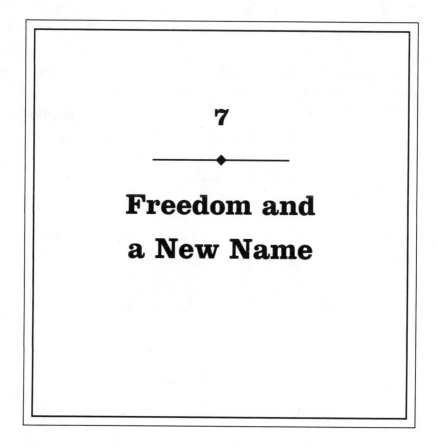

7

Freedom and a New Name

IN August, 1952, Malcolm was finally released from prison. He was released on parole, which meant that there were conditions to his being allowed to leave the prison. One of those conditions was that he have a promise of steady employment before his release. Wilfred, Malcolm's brother, worked in a furniture store in Detroit. He got the owner of the store to agree to hire Malcolm.

The first thing that Malcolm did when he left the prison

was to go to a Turkish bath. He wanted the luxury of the bath, and to clean the smell of the prison from his body.

He stayed overnight with his sister Ella, who gave him some money. In the morning he bought new glasses, a wristwatch, and a suitcase. Then he began the long bus trip from Boston to Detroit.

Malcolm was twenty-seven, and the six and a half years he had spent in prison was nearly a quarter of his life. As the bus went through city streets and along the highways of the nation's busy Northeast, he looked out and saw that the world had changed. The cars were different; the billboards advertised products he wasn't familiar with. The bus ride would last a little over twenty-four hours. His mind went back to the prison, imagining what was going on in the world behind him. He checked his watch a dozen times. It was his time now, and it was important.

Malcolm bought a newspaper at a rest stop and spent hours looking from the paper to the world around him, seeing what was considered important enough to appear in the newspapers, seeing how the people along the way looked, listening to the conversations on the bus. He wondered how he would fit into this new world.

He was glad to reach Wilfred's home, to embrace his brother, to smile, to relax, to be asked what he wanted to do. Wilfred was different than Malcolm had remembered him being. He was older, more mature, confident in what he was doing, and in his conversion to Islam.

The store in which Malcolm would work made its money from the poor. They sold cheap furniture at high prices, offering credit on which they made even more money. The store owners were the first whites that Malcolm had to deal with since he'd left prison, and he eyed them suspiciously.

He lived in Wilfred's home, and it was there that he first began learning the religious life of a Muslim. The rituals of the Muslim religion depended on disciplines that Malcolm could easily accept. Each morning he and Wilfred would rise and do their morning ablutions, a cleansing ritual that all Muslims perform. Then they would say their morning prayers. Wilfred's wife would repeat this ritual after the men in her house did, and finally the children would do so.

From the rough environment of the prison, with all of its obscenities and baseness, Malcolm was now in the calm, orderly environment of his brother's home.

Malcolm joined Temple Number One in Detroit. He was impressed by how the black people in the temple respected one another, how neatly they dressed, and how serious they were. Lemuel Hassan was the minister of Temple Number One, and he taught the other Muslims about the Islamic religion, the teachings of Elijah Muhammad, and the way of life that had been adopted by the Nation of Islam.

Malcolm entered this learning phase of his life eagerly. It was giving him a dignity he had never had before. He listened to Minister Hassan intently. He wanted to absorb as much as he could as quickly as possible.

The Detroit neighborhood in which the small temple sat was in the middle of the black ghetto. Outside, young men stood listlessly on the curb. Drunks wandered past the temple on weekends, making obscene suggestions to young sisters. There were dope pushers that drove along the streets, stopping to make an occasional drop. Malcolm recognized what they were doing. He knew what they were doing because he had lived the life.

Malcolm asked why the meetings were so poorly attended and was told that the brothers on the street were not interested in becoming Muslims, as the members of the Nation of Islam were called.

When he was a schoolboy Malcolm had been elected class president. When he was in Harlem he had been the right-hand man of some of the biggest numbers runners in town. In prison he had led debates. He was a thinker and a doer. He knew that the brothers on the street wouldn't come into the temple, giving up their whiskey and their dope, just because they saw the doors open.

Malcolm looked around the small temple and saw the empty seats. Something had to be done. There were people inside the temple who lived good, well-disciplined lives, who walked with dignity and talked of black pride. These people were doing something with their lives, while outside there were people who had become part of the mean streets on which they were living.

Malcolm spoke to Wilfred, who told him to be patient until he learned more about the Nation of Islam.

On the Sunday before Labor Day, 1952, a motorcade of ten cars left Detroit to make the trip to Chicago where Elijah Muhammad taught at Temple Number Two.

Detroit thrived on heavy industry. As the auto industry went, so went the fortunes of black people. The blacks there lived in largely segregated neighborhoods and in the poorest housing. Chicago, though, was a different story.

Jean Baptiste Point Du Sable, a black man, had helped settle the city in the late eighteenth century. Blacks lived in some of the finest homes in Chicago, and were active in all aspects of life in the busy city. Elijah Muhammad had established a temple in the Windy City in the thirties, and it was by far the most famous in the Nation of Islam. Malcolm felt a keen sense of anticipation as the small convoy of cars made its way into the city. The entire population of the Detroit Temple and the Chicago Temple combined was only two hundred people, but the meeting made a lasting impression on Malcolm.

> *I was totally unprepared for the Messenger Elijah Muhammad's physical impact upon my emotions. From the rear of Temple Number Two, he came toward the platform. The small, sensitive, gentle, brown face that I had studied on photographs, until I had dreamed about it, was fixed straight ahead as the Messenger strode, encircled by the marching, strapping Fruit of Islam guards. The Messenger, compared to them, seemed fragile, almost tiny. He and the Fruit of Islam were dressed in dark suits, white shirts, and bow ties. The Messenger wore a gold-embroidered fez.*
> —The Autobiography of Malcolm X

This was the man who had taken the time to write to Malcolm when he was in prison, who had counseled him, and had given him a way to turn his life around.

Elijah Muhammad, the Honorable Elijah Muhammad as he was called, spoke to the congregation of Muslims. He told them again that they were locked in a mortal combat with a white enemy intent upon destroying them, reducing them to a substandard existence. Black people who did not understand this, he said, were spiritually and mentally "dead."

Then Elijah Muhammad called Malcolm by name, and asked him to stand. Malcolm was stunned that he had been called by name, and nervously stood. He nodded to the black faces that turned in his direction. Elijah Muhammad spoke of the tribulations of Job. Job had been a faithful servant to God. Satan had scoffed at Job's faithfulness and said that the old man was faithful and good only because he had God's protection and blessing constantly. Satan told God that if he removed these protections Job would disappoint him.

Elijah Muhammad said that when Malcolm had been in jail he was protected from vice, and from drugs, by the walls of the prison. He said that now that Malcolm was out of jail they would see if he would be faithful to the cause of Islam.

Malcolm was thrilled. Elijah Muhammad was not only aware of his presence among the two hundred Muslims in the temple but was also challenging him personally to prove himself. It was a challenge he welcomed.

After the meeting, Elijah Muhammad invited Malcolm and others to his home. It was here that the leader of the Nation of Islam, in response to Malcolm's questions as to why the Detroit Temple was so poorly attended, suggested that the temple members try to recruit the young people in the area. Malcolm nodded, accepting for himself the job of recruiting more members.

Malcolm returned to Detroit, and began to go among the young people to bring them into the fold of Islam. This searching for new members was called "fishing for the dead."

"My man, let me pull your coat to something — " Malcolm understood the language of the streets, understood how necessary it was to let the young people he was speaking to know that he wasn't a "square." He knew what they were going through. They might have had their hair conked, might have been wearing patent leather shoes, or charcoal grays with buckles, but Malcolm could speak their language. They might have had more pride in their "shorts," the cars they had bought on credit, than in their heritage, but Malcolm knew about that, too.

Malcolm understood young black men because he had lived their lives. He understood their search for value in a society that often rejected them, because he, too, had been rejected. Malcolm understood who these young men were, and he offered them a place in which they would be valued, the Nation of Islam.

To join the Nation of Islam it was necessary to attend meetings and listen to the teachings of the ministers. Only after fully understanding the beliefs of the Nation of Islam could an application for full membership be submitted. Full membership included the right to drop one's "slave name" and the right to assume the last name of "X."

"X." The unknown, the lost African name. Somewhere between the freedom of the Mandingo warriors, the freedom of the Yoruba artists, the freedom of the Fulani herdsmen; somewhere between these freedoms and the coasts of North and South America, was a forgotten heritage, a lost language, a name no longer remembered. "X." It is a symbol of that which was lost, and that which is sought.

In 1619 a Dutch ship moored off the coast of Virginia. In its hold there were Africans who had been taken by force from their native lands. The Africans who were removed from the ship were sold to white colonists who needed their labor in the tobacco, rice, and cotton fields of the American South. This was the beginning of a long period of anguish and pain for people of African descent in North America.

The period of American slavery lasted from 1619 until the end of 1865. No people want to be enslaved, and the Africans were no different. There were bloody revolts in which many people were killed. To make the process of holding human beings easier, it was necessary to change the Africans. The plantation owners, the largest group of people who held Africans, tried to get the Africans to identify themselves not as people from the kingdoms of West Africa, where most of them had lived before being captured, but as the property of their white masters. The Africans were given new first names and were made to dress in Western clothes. They were called Negroes, even though the early plantation owners knew that some of them were Peuls, some were Yorubas, and others Hausa or Mandingo. They were also given names by the slave masters, names like Sambo, and Prince, and Robert, and Ben, and Caesar, any name that suited the whites who held them. The Africans were rarely called by two names.

Slavery was abolished by the Thirteenth Amendment to the Constitution in December of 1865, after the Civil War.

The Fourteenth Amendment to the Constitution gave citizenship to all of the newly freed Africans, and they were, from that point on, African-Americans.

There were immediate decisions that the freedmen, as they were called, had to make. One of them was what they would call themselves.

Few Africans remembered the names of their African ancestors. Most adopted the names of the people who had owned them. There were good reasons for this. During the period of slavery, families were often broken up. Children were sometimes sold away from mothers, husbands away from wives, and brothers away from sisters. Sometimes families were broken up by people being taken as "property" to settle the debts of the owners. For years after slavery ended, there were black families trying to find loved ones.

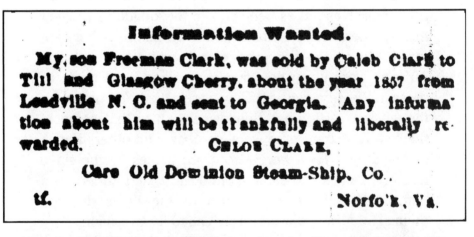

After the Civil War, many African-American families advertised for the loved ones from whom they had been separated.

If you had been sold to a plantation owner in South Carolina, and you knew you had relatives in Virginia but didn't know where they lived now that they were free, you had to have a name to look for. If your relatives had taken a completely new name, you would have no way of knowing what that name was. If they took the name of the person who had owned them, you could ask in the area if anyone knew people of that name. Still, many people referred to these names as "slave" names.

To Malcolm, the receiving of the "X" represented an important break with the life he had once led. He was, in an important sense, born again. His parents had given him the name Malcolm, but the name Little had come from the white man who had held Malcolm's ancestors during the period of black enslavement. Now Malcolm had given up Little, his slave name, and taken an X, which represented his unknown African name and symbolized the heritage that had been stolen from him.

In the Nation of Islam the X was not given lightly. Only those people who applied and were considered serious were allowed to assume this important symbol. When two members with the same first name were accepted, the first was called simply X and the second 2X. In some temples there were as many as ten people or more with the same first name, so a person might be called John 10X. But this was fine with the members of the Nation, for the names were free of the white slave masters by which outsiders were known.

Malcolm's first efforts at recruiting other members into the Nation of Islam were not particularly successful. In 1952 few blacks were prepared to hear a challenge to the idea of integration. But through persistence Malcolm's efforts paid off and the membership of the Detroit Temple tripled. In the summer of 1953 Malcolm was made an assistant minister.

It was during this period that Malcolm also visited Chicago whenever he could and talked to Elijah Muhammad. Malcolm felt humble in the presence of his spiritual leader. He respected what he had done in establishing the Nation of Islam, and saw the wisdom of his words.

"If a person has a dirty glass of water and thinks it's good," Elijah Muhammad said, "the best way to convince

Malcolm X and Elijah Muhammad

Malcolm X counseling a Nation of Islam couple

him to get rid of that water is to show him a clean glass of water."

Don't condemn, was the message, just show the best example.

Malcolm was determined not only to show, but to be the best example. Elijah Muhammad was giving Malcolm something he had never been given before: the opportunity to use his talents. What was more, he was using those talents for the betterment of his people.

Malcolm, over his lifetime, had taught himself to deal with all kinds of people. He could talk to "street" people and to college graduates. He was discovering, as were those who worked with him, that he had a genius for organizing, and a genius for reaching places in the African-American soul that organizations like the Urban League and the National Association for the Advancement of Colored People were carefully avoiding. While certain black Americans had made some gains in the United States, most young black men were doing very poorly. They were hopeless, or nearly so. Like Malcolm years before, they had "just given up."

Malcolm was made a minister and sent to Boston to help establish a temple there. He did this by contacting the Muslims already living in the city and helping them both to recruit new people and to bring them help in organizing the temple. In Boston he met some of the same people he had known when he lived there. They were shocked to see how he had changed. He was shocked to see that they had not changed. Among the Muslims in Boston there were street toughs, clerks, and even successful entertainers.

From Boston Malcolm was sent to Philadelphia. It was in Philadelphia that his father had first been involved in the Garvey movement over thirty years earlier. His success in Philadelphia was even greater than his success in Boston. In three months Temple Number Twelve had been established.

Then, in June, 1954, Malcolm was appointed the minister of Temple Number Seven in New York City. It would be his biggest challenge and his greatest opportunity. The New York Temple was a storefront in Harlem. It had only a few members, and they were not particularly effective in bringing in new members.

The year 1954 was a momentous year for African-Americans. It was a year that seemed full of promise and of fulfillment. Unemployment was at an all-time low. The Korean War had ended, and America was caught up in a love affair with Dwight David Eisenhower. The Supreme Court had declared that school segregation was unconstitutional, and to many African-Americans this signaled the end of all segregation. Many blacks viewed the problems of racism as having been "solved." But still Malcolm preached, preached on the same streets on which he had hustled numbers and reefers.

> *The white man wants black men to stay immoral, unclean and ignorant. As long as we stay in these conditions we will keep on begging him and he will control us. We never can win freedom and justice and equality until we are doing something for ourselves!*
>
> — The Autobiography of Malcolm X

Malcolm worked as hard as he could. He went wherever he was needed or requested to speak. And his message was always the same, for black people to take control of their lives by rejecting the mental and spiritual enslavement of whites, and to do those things that were in the best interests of the black race.

In the meantime, the Nation of Islam was establishing businesses in the black community. They started restau-

A Nation of Islam grocery store

rants, serving nutritious foods at reasonable prices. They opened grocery stores and encouraged their members to shop in them. Their efforts were being noted.

During the fifties the country was in the midst of a "red scare." Many people believed that the country was in danger of being taken over by communists, directed from Moscow. In 1953 the Rosenbergs, Julius and Ethel, had been executed for treason, and Senator Joseph McCarthy was investigating every phase of American intellectual life for signs of communist sympathies. J. Edgar Hoover, the head of the F.B.I., watched every movement, including the Muslims.

One of the major problems confronting the Nation of

Islam was the growing opposition of middle-class blacks. They considered the progress that blacks were making sufficient for their needs. They felt that people calling whites "blue-eyed devils" were inviting white anger and would hurt their efforts for peaceful integration.

Malcolm asked black men on street corners simply to "open their eyes" and look at the white man's history. If he wanted to give you equal opportunity, Malcolm taunted, he could have done it years ago. He was growing more and more impatient with some of his brothers.

Once, when Malcolm criticized a minister he felt was moving too slowly, Elijah Muhammad told him that he would rather have a mule that he could count on than a racehorse that was not dependable. His rapid progress within the Nation of Islam, and the speed with which he expanded the organization, would both become extremely important to Malcolm.

By 1957, the Muslims were a familiar sight in large cities, primarily in the black communities. But it was in April of 1957, with the arrest of Johnson Hinton, that the Muslims first attracted citywide attention. Hinton had complained loudly as two policemen beat a black man on a Harlem street. Hinton testified that as he walked away, one of the policemen grabbed him from the rear and started assaulting him. As Hinton tried to defend himself, other police officers joined the scuffle and clubbed Hinton to the ground. He was then taken, dazed and bleeding, to the station house.

When the word reached Temple Number Seven, Malcolm's temple, he organized a group of men and marched them to the police station. He demanded to see Hinton and then, appalled at the sight of the nearly unconscious man, demanded that he be taken to the hospital.

The story of how the Muslims had faced the police raced through the neighborhood. Being beaten by the police was not something that anyone had been able to do anything about before then. But the Muslims had faced the police, their leader had made demands, and the police had backed off! From that day on the community knew that the Nation of Islam was a force to be reckoned with.

Malcolm had devoted himself to the work he considered to be the most important thing he had done in his life. He traveled thousands of miles each month, pulling together the organization, preaching on street corners, fishing for the dead among the people he so loved. Sometimes the problems he solved dealt with renting spaces, sometimes with finding leaders to run the temples. Sometimes he dealt with complaints against the police department, and sometimes with personal problems in the lives of the members of the Nation of Islam.

Malcolm was told of a problem a particular sister had. She was studying to be a nurse, going to nursing school, and working as much as she could to support herself. Her parents were also helping in her support. When she told her parents, who were financing the bulk of her tuition costs, that she was a Muslim, they gave her an ultimatum: leave the Muslims or they would cut off the money for her nursing school.

Malcolm had seen Sister Betty X around the temple, had spoken to her briefly on several occasions. She carried herself with dignity, and had an air of seriousness about

Sister Betty X

her that Malcolm found appealing. Devoted to Islam, Betty X was also a beautiful woman, a fact that Malcolm tried to minimize as he thought about her. But he found himself thinking about her more and more, wondering how marriage to her would be.

Malcolm was shocked at the suddenness of his thoughts about Sister Betty. But later, when it was arranged that she would go to Chicago and teach there, he was glad that Elijah Muhammad had the chance to meet her. He told Malcolm that he thought she was a fine woman, and would make a good wife.

Betty X, like everybody else who dealt with Malcolm, knew that his major interests were his work. He could be stern, uncompromising, even with people he obviously liked. Personal friendships did not seem that important to him.

But sometimes, when he looked at her and his face would break into a boyish grin for no apparent reason, or when he would rearrange his long legs into a more comfortable position and lean forward to speak with her, Betty

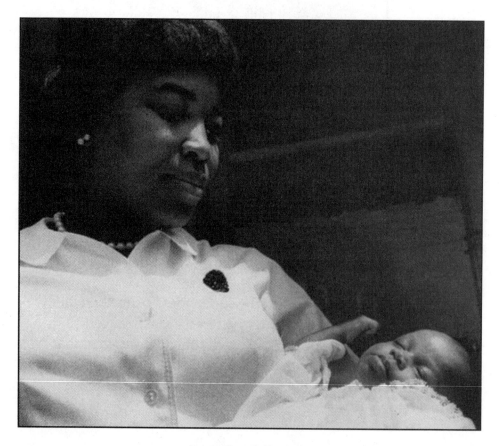

Betty X and Ilyasah

would wonder if Malcolm was more than just mildly interested in her. And as he found more and more opportunities to be with her, to sit with her at dinner, or to say some little word to her in passing, everyone else in the temple knew it, too.

When Malcolm finally made the decision to ask her to marry him, she expressed surprise. They both knew that there was something special between them, and they made that something even more special when they were married in January, 1958.

Attallah, their first daughter, was born in November of the same year. Their second daughter, Qubilah, would be born on Christmas Day, 1960. Ilyasah, a third daughter, was born in July, 1962. A fourth daughter, Gamilah, was born in 1964.

8

---◆---

Minister
Malcolm

BY EARLY 1959, Malcolm was the chief spokesperson for the Nation of Islam and its most effective minister. He had been asked by Jimmy Hicks, editor of the influential African-American paper, the *Amsterdam News*, to write a regular column. Afterwards, when Elijah Muhammad himself decided to contribute to the *Amsterdam News*, Malcolm's column was switched to another black newspaper, the *Los Angeles Herald Dispatch*. Malcolm was writing news of the Muslims, sending it into a national black newspaper, much as his mother had sent articles to *Negro World*, the Garvey newspaper. But while the *Amsterdam News* did have a desire to represent all voices in the black community, Malcolm thought it would be better if the Muslims had their own newspaper. He began the paper, which he named *Muhammad Speaks*. The paper reported on national and local news stories. It carried articles on health, education, and history as well as editorials. Soon Muslim men were selling the newspaper on the streets of every major city in the country.

The Nation of Islam itself was doing well. Its influence within the black community was spreading, and its membership rising as more and more African-Americans within the nation's troubled cities were attracted to its message and programs. One reason for the increased acceptance of the Muslims was the realization that the gains that black Americans thought would come about had simply not happened. *Brown v. The Board of Education of Topeka* had been decided in 1954 but, instead of being the quick end to segregation that some had expected, it signaled the beginning of a major resistance to integration. Blacks were still being denied the right to register and vote in many cities, and schools were still not being integrated. Black people were getting tired of waiting for equal rights.

Malcolm, in the meantime, had begun traveling throughout the world as the representative of Elijah Muhammad. Muslims in Africa and the Middle East were taking an interest in these American blacks who were fighting for their rights in the United States, and who claimed to be followers of the Islamic religion. Black people seeing newspaper articles that showed Malcolm in different countries,

Malcolm X showing a headline from the Nation of Islam newspaper,
Muhammad Speaks

talking to world leaders, realized that the Muslims were becoming more and more important. The Muslims, in the black community, were being taken more and more seriously.

Another factor attracting blacks to the Nation of Islam was that the Muslims were dealing with problems within the black community that whites were not addressing. One of these problems, in which the Muslims were particularly successful, was the fight against drug addiction.

The six-point program of the Nation of Islam was interesting from a number of perspectives. It treated drug addiction, a particular plague within the black community, as a social and racial problem as well as simply an addiction. According to Malcolm's autobiography, the program involved some steps that were similar to those used by such organizations as Alcoholics Anonymous.

First, the addict had to admit to his or her own dependence. This is an important step in the treatment of any addiction.

Second, the addict was taught, in accordance with Nation of Islam philosophy, why he or she was addicted. It was the belief of the Nation of Islam that racism in the United States had the effect of making all African-Americans feel inferior, and to feel a sense of hatred of those characteristics that made them distinct from white Americans. Drugs helped the addict to feel less pain about who he or she was.

The third step in the recovery process was to convince the addict that there was a way to recover from addiction, that addiction was not hopeless. This was an important step, as many addicts have kicked the habit for short periods of time only to find themselves back on the drug.

The fourth step was to bring the addict to the realization that he or she had the power within himself or herself to beat the drug habit.

The fifth step was to kick the habit all at once, or "cold turkey." This was done with the help of other members of the Nation of Islam who had been through the program, and whose self-esteem was high.

The sixth step was then to bring the addict into the process of healing other addicts, the message that they were bringing to other addicts being a constant reinforcement of their own break from addiction.

The success and growing popularity of the Nation of Islam was also being noticed by a number of other groups, including the F.B.I., popular magazines, newspapers, and television. Louis Lomax, a black journalist, approached Malcolm and asked if the Nation of Islam would cooperate in the filming of a television documentary about its organization. Malcolm said that he would have to refer the question to Elijah Muhammad. It was arranged for Lomax to fly to Chicago to meet with the black leader.

Elijah Muhammad understood that a television program could be an opportunity to spread the message of the Nation of Islam. It could also be a source of trouble. Muhammad knew that if the presentation was done in a way that made the Nation of Islam look good, it would attract new members, and further spread the philosophy of his organization. He also knew that although Lomax was black, the producer of the show, Mike Wallace, was white. There was a good chance that the Muslims would be shown in a very negative manner.

Elijah Muhammad became convinced that the possible

good effects of the show outweighed the possible dangers, and agreed to have the Nation of Islam cooperate. Soon, cameras were filming meetings, showing the classrooms in Muslim schools, recording speeches, and interviewing both Muslims and non-Muslims. Mike Wallace had a reputation for toughness and fairness, so Malcolm hoped for the best.

In 1959 the show was aired. It was called "The Hate That Hate Produced."

The show was edited to produce as much shock as possible. Television screens across the country were filled with images of angry black faces denouncing whites, with muscular young men training in the martial arts, with white-clad women, exotic and veiled, sitting in rows away from the Muslim men, with children learning a history that was far different from that learned by most white Americans.

There were also images of Nation of Islam restaurants and businesses, and people being treated courteously and with respect, but the overall effect of the show was shocking. Malcolm was bombarded with questions not only from across the nation, but from around the world. Were the young people in the Nation of Islam really being trained to hate white people? Were the young men, the Fruit of Islam, really being trained to fight against whites? Did the Nation of Islam think that all black people should consider all white people as the enemy? Weren't the teachings of Elijah Muhammad and his minister, Malcolm X, racist? Did black people really want to be segregated?

The reaction to "The Hate That Hate Produced" was immediate and fearful. But while the immediate reaction was to the documentary, the idea of white fear and concern about blacks had a long history of its own.

From the time that Africans were first brought to the West as a captive labor force, there had been fear and worry. Would the Africans in the fields rise up against their white masters? Could house servants be trusted not to poison the food?

In 1831, when Nat Turner led an uprising of Africans in Virginia, killing over sixty whites, the entire South was alarmed. There were millions of blacks in the South, and they had access to hand tools and scythes and other instruments that they could use as weapons. People who wanted to view blacks as simpleminded and docile were shocked. Others, who acknowledged that all men yearned for freedom, regardless of color, were not. They just wondered how many more uprisings there would be.

Whites were familiar with the civil rights movement, and most understood that blacks were not satisfied with much that was going on in the United States. They knew that blacks were still the group that was the worst off economically and received the fewest opportunities. But they were used to blacks patiently pleading their cases in courts, marching peacefully, or joining with interested whites in trying to convince others that they deserved certain rights. They were not used to the anger they saw on television, or the bitterness that was so evident.

The public wanted to know if young blacks were really being trained to hate whites. It was Malcolm, largely, who responded to newspaper and television reporters.

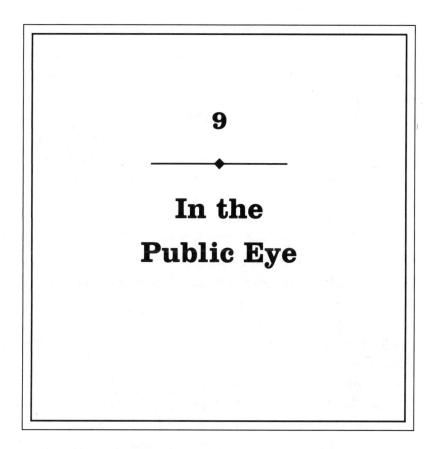

9

---◆---

In the
Public Eye

"**T**HE Hate That Hate Produced" put the Nation of Islam under a media spotlight and forced it to continue a change that had begun with the entrance of Malcolm into the movement. In the thirties and forties, the Nation had been a relatively small and closed organization designed by its leader, Elijah Muhammad, to accomplish certain ends. The first and foremost of these ends was to better the conditions of African-Americans by ridding them of their economic and psychological dependence upon white Americans.

Economic independence would take place by the building of black businesses, and by blacks spending their money within their own community. Blacks would then create jobs for other blacks and relieve the hopelessness that existed in some inner cities.

The psychological freeing was more complicated and more difficult to achieve. Elijah Muhammad understood that many blacks felt that whites were more intelligent, better-looking, and more capable than blacks. As long as they believed this, they would hate themselves. The major tools to end this psychological separation were education, a different religion, and the identification of whites as the enemy of blacks.

But before Malcolm became a very public figure, and before the Wallace documentary, Elijah Muhammad did not have to answer questions about the Nation, or about the tactics it was using. After the documentary, the entire country was examining every word that came from the Muslims.

The growth of the Muslim organization created an internal problem as well. Malcolm's robust leadership was causing a faster growth within the Nation than the structure could handle. A temple consisting of twenty or thirty members was easily manageable. But when Malcolm's recruiting increased the size of a temple to two or three hundred or even more it was difficult to find local leaders to keep the discipline and structure in line with the aims of the Nation. The Boston Temple had a young, energetic leader, Louis X, with exceptional abilities, and even he was having trouble controlling the rapid growth of his temple. Louis X would later become known as Louis Farrakhan.

In addition, Elijah Muhammad, in his mid-sixties, was beginning to experience health problems. Who would take over the leadership of the large organization? It was commonly thought that Muhammad wanted one of his sons to assume the leadership position, but Malcolm was clearly assuming that role. A clash between Elijah Muhammad and Malcolm seemed to be brewing.

Another area of possible trouble between Malcolm and the leader of the Muslims was in the basic doctrines of the Nation of Islam. Malcolm expressed interest in working with other groups, and Elijah Muhammad was against it. Malcolm wanted to use the Nation in a more active manner than his leader and teacher was willing to allow.

Malcolm, simply because he was so often the spokesman for the Muslims, often seemed to change his statements when questioned by reporters, creating some conflicts in what Elijah Muhammad publicly believed and what Malcolm seemed to believe. Louis Lomax interviewed Elijah Muhammad in 1959:

> *Mr. Lomax: Now, you have on the other hand said that the devil is the white man — that the white man is a doomed race.*
> *Mr. Elijah Muhammad: Yes.*
> *Mr. Lomax: Am I correct there, sir?*
> *Mr. Elijah Muhammad: Yes.*

In a public speech, Malcolm seemed to deliver the same message:

Our enemy is the white man! . . . Oh, yes, that devil is our enemy.

Did Malcolm believe that the white man was the devil? Did he really believe, during this period of his life, that all whites were evil?

It can be said that Malcolm came upon the Nation of Islam at a critical time in his life. He needed the discipline and the precision of the Nation of Islam and was willing to cooperate with Elijah Muhammad and his beliefs, even though Malcolm himself probably accepted some of the details of Muhammad's teachings as more symbolic than factual. There was no doubt that Elijah Muhammad did not believe, literally, some of the things that the Muslims said. Yet he did believe that the strategy of hostility to whites was the most useful one for African-Americans. But as Malcolm developed with the Nation of Islam, his ideas grew stronger, and his speeches became more and more his own and less the speeches of the Nation of Islam.

As reporters, white and black, tried to pin down Malcolm to specific issues and questions, he avoided many questions by referring to the symbolism of the statements made by the Nation of Islam.

Malcolm's message of separation from whites was very disturbing to black leaders from the broad middle class, who were in the forefront of the civil rights movement. Their feeling was that there would be an eventual acceptance of black rights by whites. Malcolm's demand for immediate full equality, and for freedom, "by any means necessary," challenged the orderly process toward civil rights that many black leaders had planned. They were trying to portray African-Americans as an orderly, peaceful people who were unjustly denied their rights and who wanted to fit into the American mainstream. The Nation of Islam was not only rejecting the American mainstream but was threatening to disrupt the social order "by any means necessary" if blacks did not get what they wanted.

Many whites worked in the civil rights movement; some had been beaten and others had been killed as they joined the black protest. But in his speeches, Malcolm rejected any solution to the problems of black Americans that involved their fitting into a white society.

Revolution is bloody, revolution is hostile, revolution knows no compromise, revolution overturns and destroys everything that gets in its way.

Liberals were also against the policies of the Nation of Islam because it prevented coalitions in which whites would be participating. Whites were heavily involved in organizations such as the N.A.A.C.P. and the Urban League. They had proven helpful and even vital to these organizations. Now they were being rejected by the Nation of Islam.

But young blacks, especially young black males, often admired Malcolm even if they did not agree completely with the ideas he offered. They liked his idea of gaining freedom "by any means necessary." They did not want to wait another hundred years until all the court cases had been won, and all the conditions were "right" for black progress. What's more, they wanted to feel as if they were standing up for their own rights, not begging for them.

Elijah Muhammad, although sometimes troubled by Malcolm's statements and his impatience, recognized Malcolm's enormous gifts and tolerated their differences.

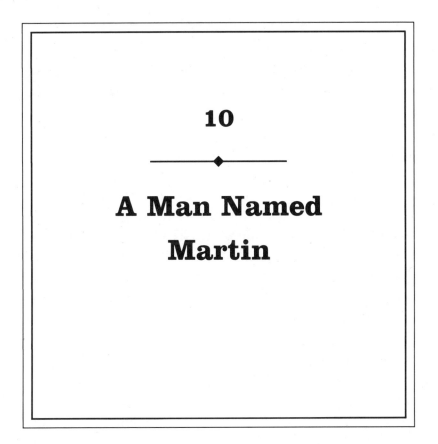

10

◆

A Man Named
Martin

NO ONE stands alone in history. Earl Little, Malcolm's father, lived during the era of Marcus Garvey. Garvey's ideas and leadership influenced the Little family. Before Garvey there were Booker T. Washington and William E. B. Du Bois. Before all of these men there was the fiery Frederick Douglass, and before Douglass there were others, some free, some enslaved, who sought freedom and equality for their people.

Even when he was most active, creating a style and form

of leadership that would inspire others, Malcolm was being compared to other black leaders of this period. The most notable of these was Martin Luther King, Jr.

During the period of African enslavement, the "owners" understood very clearly that the Africans did not want to work in their fields, or to be held in bondage. Afraid that they were making plans to rise up against them, plantation owners tried to keep the blacks from gathering in groups when they were not supervised. The only exceptions to this, and this was allowed only in some cases, were religious meetings. Few Africans had retained a major body of knowledge about African religions, and most adopted the Christianity they had been introduced to in the South.

The expression of their religious beliefs was important to African-Americans. Sometimes, for families barely surviving on rural tenant farms or in urban tenements, it was the only way to release the emotions that filled them: emotions of sorrow, of joy, of reverence for a Supreme Being.

In the black community, the man of God, the man who could give voice to the yearnings and fears of his people, was highly respected.

There were few other fields that afforded blacks a leadership role. Some preachers, like Earl Little, had only a few followers and preached their sermons wherever they could, sometimes in churches that needed a minister for a short time, sometimes in small rooms borrowed for the purpose. Other preachers, usually those in large cities, managed either to buy or build large churches and preached to hundreds of people each week. Successful preachers could often rally entire communities around their ministry and, by careful leadership, could influence local governments to some extent. The communities, in turn, often looked toward men of daring and intelligence to be the heads of their churches.

Malcolm began his ministry in the Islamic religion in the big cities of the North: Detroit, Philadelphia, Boston, and New York. While he was spreading the word of the Nation of Islam there were other black movements going on around the country, movements that would bring forth other leaders.

Jim Crow laws, those laws that allowed cities and states to prevent blacks from enjoying the same privileges as whites, were prevalent throughout the South in the fifties. Blacks were forbidden to drink from the same fountains as whites, were not allowed to sit with whites in theaters, were not allowed to eat in restaurants reserved for whites only, or even to share public facilities with whites.

One particular law said that blacks had to sit in the rear of buses. Some buses had special sections marked "colored," while in others it was just understood that blacks sat in the rear, while whites sat in the front. The usual result of Jim Crow laws was that blacks had poorer facilities than whites, or none at all.

In Montgomery, Alabama, the law said that blacks sat in the rear of the bus, moving toward the front as the rear of the bus filled. But if the white section of the bus filled, then blacks sitting nearer the front would have to get up and give their seats to any whites who boarded the bus, standing if there were no other seats available.

On the first day of December, 1955, a smallish black woman sat down near the center of a nearly empty bus in Montgomery. Rosa Parks had just come from work and was on her way home. She was told by the driver to get up and move to the rear of the bus to allow a white man to sit in her seat. She had paid the same amount of money as the white rider and refused to give up her seat. It was against the law, in Montgomery, for a black person to refuse to give up a seat when told to do so, and Rosa Parks was arrested.

The Supreme Court had already ruled the year before,

Dr. Martin Luther King, Jr., led the Montgomery, Alabama, boycott against segregated buses.

in the Brown decision, that school segregation was unconstitutional. The Court had ruled that when black children went to segregated schools they were hurt because segregation itself injured them. Lawyers thought that other cases involving segregation would have to be tried before all segregation was officially ended.

When the black community of Montgomery discovered that Rosa Parks had been arrested, it decided to fight the case both in the streets and in the courts. The black leadership in Montgomery understood that the case could be an important one with a lot of press coverage, and they needed a leader who could handle both the planned boycott of the buses and the press. After much discussion, they decided on a young minister who had recently moved to Montgomery from Georgia.

Martin Luther King, Jr., was born on the fifteenth of January, 1929, in Atlanta, Georgia. His grandfather on his mother's side, Adam Daniel Williams, had founded the Ebenezer Baptist Church in Atlanta in 1894. Martin's father had taken over the church in 1931, and it was under his leadership that the church became one of the most important black churches in Georgia. Martin Luther King, Sr., fought for the rights of black people in Atlanta and was a leading member of the N.A.A.C.P.

Young Martin was a good student, skipping several grades in high school and entering Morehouse College in Atlanta at the age of fifteen. In 1948 he received a bachelor's degree from Morehouse and went on to Crozer Theological Seminary in Pennsylvania.

The idea of the boycott was simple. The public transportation system in Montgomery depended on the fares of all its riders, black and white. Without the blacks of Montgomery riding the buses and paying their fares, the bus company would lose money on a daily basis.

The Montgomery boycott had another advantage that few black protests had had in the past: television. Instead of the struggle between blacks and whites being isolated within a community, the protesters were seen throughout the nation, and eventually throughout the world. Martin Luther King, Jr., was seen on television, carefully, but with great passion, explaining the position of the boycotters. His nonviolent approach helped to bring sympathy to the movement, and he emerged from the successful boycott as the most famous black man in the United States.

Dr. King's philosophy of nonviolence had two major effects. The first was to create enormous sympathy for the black cause throughout the world. The second was to increase moral pressure on American legislators to pass and enforce the new civil rights laws.

While Dr. King's tactics were nonviolent, the resistance against the growing civil rights movement was far from nonviolent. Civil rights workers were frequently attacked. Sometimes the attacks were mild, sometimes they were extremely violent. Dr. King himself was put into jail, and his home was bombed.

Black students who "sat-in" at lunch counters reserved for whites only under the Jim Crow laws were humiliated, and had food and condiments thrown on their clothing and heads. Racist mobs ridiculed the nonviolent protesters.

Schoolchildren who attempted to enroll at previously all-white schools were being barred at the school doors or harassed to the point that they did not wish to risk being hurt by attending the schools.

Dr. King vowed "to carry on nonviolent crusades against the evils of second-class citizenship throughout the South."

In May, 1957, when New Yorkers were talking about the strength of Malcolm X and the Nation of Islam, people in the South were talking about the strength of Martin Luther King, Jr., and nonviolence. Two men, one in the South, the other in the North. Both of them represented areas of the

Nonviolent acts of civil disobedience characterized the civil rights movement under Dr. King.

black experience. Martin Luther King, Jr., with roots deeply planted in Georgia soil, represented a more traditional approach. His was the leadership of Christianity and non-violence. Malcolm, whose father and grandfather had come from Georgia as well, also represented the black experience. Blacks before Malcolm, men such as Nat Turner, Denmark Vesey, and Gabriel Prosser, had resorted to violence or the threat of violence to obtain their rights.

Both men were involved with their respective religions. Dr. King's advocacy of nonviolence was in the tradition of idealistic Christianity and the teachings of Gandhi, the Indian leader. Martin Luther King, Jr., marshaled not only the members of his own church but members of other Christian churches as well.

Malcolm X could direct not only his own temple under the guidance of Elijah Muhammad, but temples throughout the country.

Many strategists believed that Dr. King's philosophy was particularly suited to the South, where the oppression of black people was worst and the possibility of retaliatory violence was much greater. Even the threat of black-on-white violence would have greatly increased the amount of people injured and killed. Dr. King also realized that the Jim Crow laws were beginning to be an embarrassment to the American government. Americans were having trouble calling themselves the world's greatest democracy when they allowed the public humiliation of American citizens just because of their color.

But the Nation of Islam, and Malcolm X, took a different view of American history. The United States had been

Malcolm X leading a rally

created as a democracy that aspired to freedom while slavery existed within its borders.

The differences between Martin Luther King, Jr., and Malcolm X were primarily in their methods. Both men were dedicated to bettering the condition of their people. But there were major differences in how they were perceived by the outside world. Dr. King seemed, at least to liberal whites, to be a reasonable man, a man who had a higher moral purpose than most and whose cause was just. Non-violence pointed up blacks as people who only wanted to exercise their rights as Americans.

Day in and day out the television news showed students

and black protesters being beaten or assaulted with fire hoses. Under Dr. King, blacks sat-in, and prayed-in, and asked the courts to assume their cases.

To Malcolm there was no need to change the moral plane of the movement, or to seek white sympathizers. If African-Americans did not have the same rights as whites, he reasoned, it was only because whites did not want to grant those rights. He said:

> *We are humbling ourselves, sitting-in, and beg-ging-in, trying to unite with the slavemaster!*

**In Birmingham, Alabama, police used water cannons
against civil rights demonstrators.**

. . . the white man is telling you, "You can't live here, you can't enter here, you can't eat here, drink here, walk here, you can't ride here, you can't play here, you can't study here." Haven't we yet seen enough to see that he had no plan to unite with you?

For all of his public life Malcolm was compared to Martin Luther King, Jr. It was a comparison that Malcolm ac-

Dr. King and Malcolm X at their one meeting

ITY INFORMATION—CON...NTIAL

FEDERAL BUREAU OF INVESTIGATION

REPORT MADE AT	DATE WHEN MADE	PERIOD FOR WHICH MADE	REPORT MADE BY
BOSTON	MAY 4 1953	3/20:4/1,3,6/'53	BA

TITLE

MALCOLM K. LITTLE, was.
Malachi Shabazz; "Rythun Red"; Detroit Red;

CHARACTER OF CASE

SECURITY MATTER-C
SECURITY MATTER-MCI

SYNOPSIS OF FACTS:

Subject resides at 4336 Williams Street, Inkster, Michigan. Subject claimed in June, 1950, that he was a Communist and during September, 1952, he indicated membership in the Muslim Cult of Islam.

-RUC-

DETAILS:- This investigation was predicated upon informa- tion received from

Norfolk, had written two letters Subject. included comments on Communism;

ALL INFORMATION CONTAINED HEREIN IS UNCLASSIFIED
DATE

I. BACKGROUND

Birth

was born May 19, 1925, in Omaha, Nebraska, and is a citizen by virtue of his birth

COPIES DESTROYED
JUL 23 1962

Employment

Information received from Boston Informant

APPROVED AND FORWARDED

SPECIAL AGENT IN CHARGE

DO NOT WRITE IN THESE SPACES

COPY IN FILE

COPIES OF THIS REPORT

5 Bureau
4-Detroit(100-21719
1-25-17462)
2-Boston (100-27649)

100-399324

SE-15

MAY 8 1953

PROPERTY OF FBI—This confidential report and its contents are loaned to you by the FBI and are not to be distributed outside of agency to which loaned.

MAY 20 1953

The F.B.I.'s file on Malcolm X

cepted, for it pointed out the differences between the Nation of Islam and the traditional black protest movement that King represented. Dr. King urged blacks to maintain their own humanity in the face of white oppression, to love whites as brothers, despite discrimination and violence.

Malcolm said it was ridiculous for black men to "turn the other cheek" when their women and children were being beaten and killed. Hostility was the only language, he said, that some people understood.

Malcolm knew that he was considered the "bad man" of the black movement and that King was considered to be the good one. He relished his "bad" image.

What both men had in common—with each other, with Malcolm's father, with Marcus Garvey, and with other African-Americans in the long struggle for civil rights since the early twenties—was scrutiny by the Federal Bureau of Investigation. The F.B.I. understood that both men were effective leaders and wondered just where they would take the black movement.

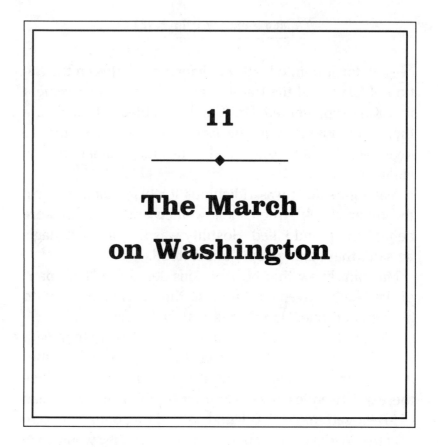

11

◆

The March
on Washington

SEPTEMBER, 1960. Malcolm was, by now, well known. Young black men quoted him on street corners. But how important a leader was Malcolm? African-Americans in the inner cities were watching him, wondering what he would do next, where he would lead the movement. There were others watching as well. The F.B.I. had started a file on Malcolm. Paid black informants reported his most private conversations.

But while Malcolm was considered, in the United States,

to be a leader of some blacks and some vague organization known as the Nation of Islam, he was also being seen by some as a revolutionary. One of those who saw Malcolm as both a revolutionary and a possible ally in the United States was Fidel Castro, the Cuban leader.

Fidel Castro was born in Oriente Province, Cuba, on the thirteenth of August, 1926. He was born in a Cuba that for years had been under the influence of the United States, and which had oppressed the poor of that nation. Castro, after a long and difficult campaign, overthrew the government of Fulgencio Batista in 1959. The United States had supported Castro's struggle against the Batista dictatorship until, when he came to power, he declared himself a communist.

Castro was an able leader and an inspiring speaker. After taking over the government of Cuba he took over the American sugar business in his country and aligned himself with the worldwide communist movement. In September, 1960, he came to the United States to address the United Nations. A Cuban who had fled Batista talked about his feelings for Fidel Castro:

> *He is wonderful, man. When he speaks his strength is in his words, his mouth. He speaks for the little people of Cuba.*

The Federal Bureau of Investigation had already been keeping tabs on Malcolm by paying informants within the Nation of Islam. Their attention was not on Malcolm, however, when Castro came to the United States. Castro, in violently taking over the government of Cuba, had made enemies, and the government did not want anything to happen to him in the United States. Secure hotels were suggested to his party, but were rejected. Where would he stay?

When Fidel Castro announced that he would stay in Harlem, in the Hotel Theresa, there was an uproar. Security arrangements had to be switched from midtown, where Castro had been expected to stay, to the Harlem location.

In Harlem there was an air of excitement. Presidents had whizzed through Harlem, waving from fast-moving cars, and other government officials had made brief visits to Harlem, but no world leader had deliberately chosen the black community as his headquarters.

The Hotel Theresa had been the gathering place and

The Hotel Theresa in Harlem

temporary residence of the most famous Harlemites. Joe Louis had stayed there, as had Nat King Cole, and Sugar Ray Robinson. The bottom floors of the hotel housed a bar and a beauty salon. There were single rooms with no view and suites with balconies that overlooked the vibrant Harlem community.

The newspapers had announced that Castro and his entourage would stay in the Theresa, and the streets around the hotel were jampacked with African-Americans searching the balconies for a glimpse of the Cuban leader. The police department at first tried to keep the streets clear but soon gave up as the milling crowd grew from hundreds to thousands.

"You'll recognize him by his uniform!" was the rumor.

According to radio reports, Premier Castro still wore the uniform he wore in the jungles outside of Havana when he fought with his brother and Che Guevara against Batista's army.

Another rumor started circulating—that the Cubans had brought live chickens into the hotel from "La Marqueta," the Spanish-American market area under the tracks in Spanish Harlem. Some thought that this rumor was just being spread to discredit the revolutionary leader.

Malcolm and a few members of the Nation of Islam were also in the hotel. He sent a representative to the Cuban representatives.

Fidel Castro, in Cuba, had heard of Malcolm. The American press had made sure of that. Would he speak to the head of Temple Number Seven? The answer was a resounding yes!

The F.B.I., by this time, had informants who stayed close

to Malcolm, agreeing with his statements and trying to stay within his good graces so they could report back to the Bureau.

When Malcolm went to visit Premier Castro, however, the informant was not present at the meeting, and had to discuss what had happened with Malcolm later. On the twenty-first of September the informant told the F.B.I. that Malcolm had told Premier Castro that when he saw a man that the United States was against, then he knew that there was probably something good about that man.

The Cuban premier had replied that the people of the United States were not against him, only the government.

The Bureau document went on to discuss Malcolm's reason for visiting Premier Castro, which was that he was on a committee that had been formed to meet and greet delegates to the United Nations who came to Harlem.

The Nation of Islam, Malcolm said, was basically a religious organization, which could not form a partnership with a communist nation that did not accept the existence of a God.

Meeting with Fidel Castro

But the important aspect of Malcolm's meeting with Castro was the fact that it had happened at all. The Bureau had already identified Castro as an important enemy of the United States. Cuba was only minutes by air from the Florida coast, and Castro was inviting Russian technicians into the small country.

Although the F.B.I. informant reported that the meeting between Castro and Malcolm had not been preplanned, it was obvious that it had been. Castro had moved to the Hotel Theresa to make a point, that he was sympathetic to the cause of blacks in the United States.

An alliance between dissatisfied African-Americans and a communist country that had a large black population was viewed as a threat to national security, especially by the Federal Bureau of Investigation.

By March, 1961, special agents of the F.B.I. were attending all of Malcolm's speeches. Malcolm knew that there were informants within the Nation of Islam and claimed that some of them had admitted as much to him. The possibility of anyone admitting to Malcolm that he was an F.B.I. informant was highly unlikely. But Malcolm began to refer to the agents, whom he suspected to be black, in his speeches. Later, on a Washington, D.C., television program, he said:

> *The F.B.I. spends twenty-four hours a day infiltrating or trying to infiltrate Muslims and after we hold our religious services they go from door to door and ask questions of persons who come to the meetings to try to harass and frighten them.*

During 1962 and early 1963, the F.B.I. continued to watch Malcolm, attending all of his public appearances, and paying special attention to the friction between Malcolm and the sons of Elijah Muhammad.

The health of Elijah Muhammad was becoming more and more precarious. People close to him in the Nation of Islam did not expect him to be able to continue as the head of the Muslim organization for very long. Muhammad wanted his sons to take over the Nation, but realized that Malcolm would be a strong contender for the leadership.

Meanwhile, the civil rights movement was in crisis. In Birmingham, Alabama, the public safety commissioner was Eugene "Bull" Connor. "Bull" Connor was determined to stop any pro-civil rights actions by blacks in his city. When blacks attempted to demonstrate, he had hundreds, including students and children, hauled off to local jails. In addition, he used police dogs and fire hoses to disperse crowds of young black people. President John F. Kennedy privately said that the brutality that "Bull" Connor displayed would do more to promote support for civil rights than anything he, as president, could have done. The violence against blacks in Birmingham continued, and the mood in Birmingham was getting uglier and uglier. Finally, the blacks had had enough and began to confront the Birmingham police. President Kennedy saw a possibly disastrous situation. He directed that troops move into Birmingham to keep the peace.

All over the world there were reports on what was happening in the United States. The communist countries were playing and replaying scenes from the confrontations in Birmingham.

When President Kennedy sent a routine message to the Conference of Independent African Nations that merely agreed with the stated aims of the conference, namely African unity, Prime Minister Milton Obote sent back a scathing reply that condemned racism in Birmingham.

President Kennedy did not want to have demonstrations and confrontations across the United States. He decided to sponsor civil rights legislation, which was quickly opposed by southern congressmen.

The anger that black America was feeling in 1963 was at a boiling point. The Kennedy administration wondered just where it would go. The southerners who wanted to go slow on integration, who wanted to ease their way into change, had time-tested methods of preventing laws from being passed. They could simply prevent votes from ever taking place by not ending the debates on issues. Then, either the government would come to a complete halt, or whatever bill they wanted to prevent from passing would be put aside.

It was then that blacks began to talk about a march on the nation's capital.

There had been other marches on Washington. After the First World War there had been a march of veterans that filled the streets of the capital. Other groups had protested, mostly peacefully. But a black march on Washington, especially an angry march that threatened to be violent, was surely not something the government wanted.

The Kennedy administration called in black leaders and black thinkers, and asked for advice. The advice was that black America was angry, and something needed to be done, and done quickly. It was clear that Martin Luther

King, Jr.'s, policy of nonviolence was not what angry blacks around the country were interested in hearing.

The Nation of Islam is often called the "Black Muslims." And although they preached nonaggression, it was always felt, among blacks and whites, that the threat of violence lay just beneath the surface of their actions. If Martin Luther King, Jr., could get thousands of blacks to pray and protest peacefully, it was feared that Malcolm might get that many to tear America apart.

President Kennedy first tried to stop the march, but then, once he saw that blacks were actually organizing it, encouraged the march under the nonviolent leadership supported by the administration.

Malcolm was furious. First, he was furious that the "traditional" black leadership had helped the administration change a march of angry and determined people into what he called a "farce on Washington." Then he was angry that the black leaders had accepted whites as leaders of the march.

As the march took shape, it seemed that Malcolm was right in his predictions. Members of the Student Nonviolent Coordinating Committee (S.N.C.C.) who had been active in the sit-ins throughout the South, had prepared a speech. But the speech was viewed by some white clergymen as being too hostile and it was changed. The signs that marchers were allowed to carry were cleared through a committee that made sure they weren't offensive. Every detail of the march was planned, much of it by whites. When Malcolm, who went to Washington as an observer, heard about the arguments between the black students who wanted to take a more militant stance and the whites

The March on Washington

who were participating in the march, he repeated his charge, made before he went to Washington, that whites were using the blacks as "puppets."

Finally, the day of the march came. The twenty-eighth of August, 1963, was a gloriously bright and sunny day for the largest civil rights demonstration the United States had ever seen. Over a quarter of a million people from all over the country traveled to Washington, D.C. There were whites and blacks, rich and poor, trade union members, politicians, athletes, ministers, people from all walks of life, many of whom had never participated in any civil rights demonstration before.

To some, the March on Washington turned out to be a

well-orchestrated and enormous outpouring of support for civil rights. To others, it turned out to be simply a grand picnic, an overblown "feel good" session rescued only by the stirring speech of Martin Luther King, Jr. His "I Have a Dream" speech, made on the steps of the Lincoln Memorial, turned the day into a memorable experience. One of King's advisors, Stanley Levison, said:

> . . . it was marvelous in Martin's speech the way he handled the white and Negro question, completely repudiating this kind of nonsense of Adam Powell and the Muslims . . .

Adam Clayton Powell, Jr., and Malcolm X

Adam Clayton Powell, Jr., was a black congressman from Harlem who, like Malcolm, did not believe that demonstrations of support such as the March on Washington would bring about real change.

Less than three weeks later, on a Sunday morning, the fifteenth of September, Sunday school was being held at the Sixteenth Street Baptist Church in Birmingham. In the women's class the topic was "The Love That Forgives." Suddenly there was a tremendous noise and the entire building was shaken. Adult men were tossed about, chairs overturned. There were violent screams of agony, and softer moans. Women ignored their own pain as they searched through the rubble for their children. People were being put into cars and taken to hospitals. The wail of ambulances cut through the morning air.

Four black children were killed in the bombing.

In another part of the city, a thirteen-year-old black boy was shot to death by a young white boy returning home from a segregationist meeting. King's supporters were angry. They told him that he could not preach nonviolence in the face of the deaths of black children and not have some positive plan, some actions, that blacks could take to move forward. King was deeply hurt by the bombings. Still, he adhered to his policy of nonviolence and began making plans for a massive voting campaign.

The violence against blacks was overwhelming and, seemingly, growing. Increasingly it was Malcolm's voice that African-Americans were hearing as the voice of reason. How could you turn the other cheek when your children were being killed?

12

The Split with Elijah Muhammad

WITHIN the Nation of Islam the split between Malcolm and Elijah Muhammad was becoming more pronounced, more difficult to handle. Muhammad was still limiting his statements to the core philosophy of the Nation of Islam, while Malcolm was talking about international issues. Increasingly, when some incident occurred either in the United States or abroad, the media was turning to Malcolm for a response. Elijah Muhammad was more than willing to allow the more widely read Malcolm to speak for the Nation of Islam. It was Malcolm, not Muhammad, who could challenge even the most experienced debaters on television or on college campuses, and it was Malcolm who seemed to have his finger on the pulse of what was happening in the country. It was Malcolm who had challenged the organization of the March on Washington, and Malcolm who had responded most forcefully to the Birmingham bombings. Muhammad was often put in the position of being asked if he agreed with Malcolm.

Muhammad realized that Malcolm was a dynamic speaker, and he was a younger man with enormous energy. Betty X saw her husband always on the go, always traveling to teach or to act as a spokesman for the Nation of Islam. Malcolm often felt that he did not spend enough time with his family, although the time he did spend with his young wife and daughters were times of great warmth and tenderness. But Betty knew how important his work was, too. They would go to the beach, and she would find herself playing with the children as Malcolm worked over a speech, or considered a strategy for an upcoming meeting. The children knew little of their father's work, and were surprised to see news clips of him on television when he was home.

Malcolm, since his release from prison, had dedicated his life to the Nation of Islam. He had brought the Nation from a relatively small, loosely organized group to one of the most powerful political forces in America. It was not simply the membership that made it a potent group, but the composition of that membership. The large body of highly disciplined and openly militant black men and women, ready to respond at a moment's notice to any emergency, and under the leadership of a fiery leader, was something the United States had not seen before. The Nation of Islam claimed not to encourage violence, but people listening to Malcolm weren't sure, especially when he pointed out to black men that they had not been non-violent in the wars that Americans had fought overseas.

"Why," he challenged, "are you going to be nonviolent when they bomb your churches, and kill your children?"

The United States was waiting for the answer.

But Malcolm had also grown over the years he had been with the Nation. He felt he could lead the Muslims into a more active role than the one selected by Elijah Muhammad. He still claimed to believe in the basic philosophy of Elijah Muhammad, but had his own ideas as well. In fact, he had not grown beyond the Nation of Islam so much as in a different direction.

There were constant rumors about and around the Nation of Islam. Some of the sources of the rumors were clear, others were not. But one of the rumors that had been circulating in the early summer of 1963 was that Elijah Muhammad was the father of several children by women to whom he was not married. This was a violation of the principles of the Muslims.

In July, 1963, the Los Angeles papers had reported that the sixty-seven-year-old Muhammad was facing two paternity suits.

Malcolm also was having problems with the internal running of the Nation. He recognized that the Muslims were asking for financial support from people who could scarcely pay their rent. There was talk of people being intimidated.

Malcolm X in conference with Elijah Muhammad

Many of the problems, indirectly, were Malcolm's fault. He had expanded the Nation faster than the Nation could expand its leadership capabilities. Elijah Muhammad had made him a national minister, but was refusing to give him the full authority to reorganize the Nation.

Instead, Malcolm was asked several times to tone down his remarks. Muhammad realized that the scrutiny the Nation was getting in the press needed careful handling, and that Malcolm's style was anything but careful. When Medgar Evers, the head of the N.A.A.C.P. in Mississippi, was assassinated in the summer of 1963, it was all the Nation of Islam could do to keep Malcolm calm. Malcolm was further enraged when the little girls were killed in Birmingham.

Malcolm wrote to Elijah Muhammad and asked to talk to him about the infidelities that were charged. Elijah Muhammad invited Malcolm to the Arizona home where he had gone to live because of his health.

When Malcolm arrived at Elijah's home in Phoenix the two men embraced, as they always had.

"Well, son," Muhammad said, "what is on your mind?"

Malcolm told Elijah Muhammad what was being said about him, and that he, Malcolm, wanted to teach that a man's accomplishments were more important than his weaknesses.

Elijah seemed to agree with Malcolm.

Malcolm was clearly disappointed in the man who had been his advisor and mentor, and of whom he had once said:

> *He was The Messenger of Allah. When I was a foul, vicious convict, so evil that other convicts called me Satan, this man had rescued me. He was the man who had trained me, who had treated me as if I were his own flesh and blood. He was the man who had given me wings — to go places, to do things I otherwise never would have dreamed of. We walked, with me caught up in a whirlwind of emotions.*
>
> — The Autobiography of Malcolm X

Malcolm was disappointed, but so was Elijah Muhammad, who saw Malcolm as turning against him.

Malcolm returned to New York and continued to speak both to Nation of Islam meetings and to answer questions about the civil rights movement.

At this time, the country was getting more involved in the Vietnam War, and Malcolm made several statements about the possible involvement of the United States in the assassination of two Vietnamese officials.

Black leaders in the N.A.A.C.P. and the S.N.C.C. were trying to head off more violence and confrontations, including King's nonviolent confrontations, until they came up with a new strategy. President Kennedy was trying to appeal to southern politicians behind the scenes. His advisors doubted the wisdom of his traveling to Dallas, but he decided to make the trip.

Friday, the twenty-second of November, 1963. The presidential motorcade made its way slowly through the Dallas streets. In the open car President Kennedy sat next to his wife, Jackie. John Connally, Governor of Texas, sat in front of him. Suddenly there was a series of shots. A secret service agent ran around the back of the car. Kennedy's head jerked back. Jackie Kennedy reacted physically, moving almost out of the car. The President of the United States had been assassinated.

It was a bitterly cold day in New York when the news came that the President had been murdered. The first thing that blacks wanted to know was if a black man had been accused of killing him. When it was discovered that Lee Harvey Oswald, a white man, had been accused, there was a collective sigh of relief, followed by a feeling of sincere grief. John F. Kennedy had been the most popular president among blacks since Franklin Roosevelt.

The ministers of the Nation of Islam received instructions not to comment on the assassination.

Elijah Muhammad had a speaking engagement on Monday, the first of December, which he canceled. Malcolm was told to speak in his place. When he had finished speaking he was immediately questioned about the assassination of the President.

Malcolm said that the President had allowed the assassination of South Vietnamese President Ngo Dinh Diem and his brother. He said that the President "never foresaw that the chickens would come home to roost so soon."

Malcolm claimed later that he felt that the atmosphere of violence in the United States had been tolerated by the administration, and that it was this atmosphere that had finally claimed the life of the President. But the statement was interpreted by the press, and a grieving nation, as showing pleasure over the death of Kennedy.

Malcolm was officially silenced by Elijah Muhammad. The press was notified that Malcolm would not be allowed to speak for ninety days.

Malcolm accepted the discipline. He felt hurt, and betrayed.

"I felt as though something in *nature* had failed," he said, "like the sun, or the stars."

Malcolm had met a young boxer, Cassius Clay, two years earlier. He had seen him at a number of Muslim meetings. He knew him to be interested in the Nation of Islam. Clay invited Malcolm and his family to his fight camp in Miami.

Clay was the underdog in a match against the then heavyweight champion of the world, Sonny Liston. Liston, a huge man, seemed invincible. Clay didn't look nearly as menacing as the older boxer. The former Olympic champion was young, brash, and handsome. While Clay trained for the fight, Malcolm struggled with his strained relations with the Nation of Islam.

The night of the fight, the twenty-fifth of February, 1964, Malcolm sat in seat number seven for the preliminary fights. Before the fight started, he went to Clay's dressing room and joined him for a moment of silent prayer.

The actual fight started as expected, with the doleful Liston stalking the younger Clay. Between the fourth and fifth rounds it looked as if the fight would be stopped as

Malcolm X with heavyweight champion Cassius Clay, who changed his name to Muhammad Ali

Clay claimed that he had got something in his eyes and couldn't see. But Clay did continue and scored a seventh round knockout that stunned the sports world.

After the fight, Clay went to Malcolm's motel and there was a party during which Clay ate ice cream and joked with his supporters. Malcolm photographed the young champion. At the press conference the next day Clay made a confession of faith in the religion of Islam. He would later change his name to Muhammad Ali.

There was a frenzy of excitement. Now there were two black men, both young, articulate, and attractive, both national figures, who had adopted the religion of Islam.

As expected, there were negative reactions. People who prided themselves on being tolerant of all religions attacked Clay.

Malcolm returned to New York where he heard more negative stories about himself and his "betrayal" of Elijah Muhammad. He wondered what he should do. Death threats were received from sources that could not be ignored. He was working on a book with Alex Haley, the black writer who had interviewed him for *Playboy* magazine. Haley noted that Malcolm looked tired.

Malcolm was more than tired, he was physically and mentally drained. But even though he was extremely exhausted he understood what the rumors meant, that the Nation of Islam was finished with him. He decided that the only logical course of action for him was to make the break as cleanly as possible. On the eighth of March, 1964, he announced his split from the Nation of Islam.

Malcolm X announces his split from the Nation of Islam.

There was a flurry of F.B.I. memos from New York to Washington as *The New York Times* reported the story on the front page. Other papers across the nation did the same. On the twelfth of March, Malcolm announced the formation of an organization called the Muslim Mosque, Incorporated.

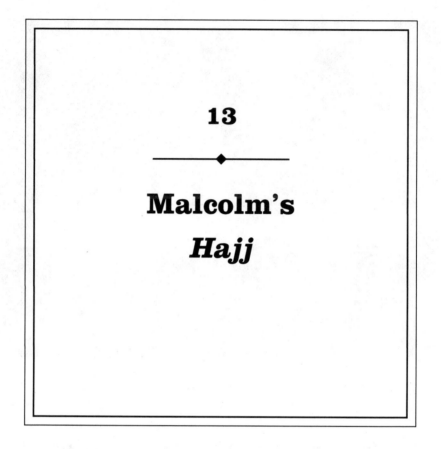

13

Malcolm's *Hajj*

MALCOLM was disappointed about his separation from the Nation of Islam, but he was prepared to move on. The Muslim Mosque, Incorporated, was to be a political organization dedicated to helping African-Americans. But a good part of what had made Malcolm leave the Nation of Islam was the worsening moral climate he sensed within the organization. At the time he understood, from the way that information was being leaked to the white press, and by the way that even private conversations seemed to find their way into the public sector, that the Nation of Islam had been infiltrated by some police agency. There was no way for him to know how much of the information he had received about Elijah Muhammad was being generated by infiltrators. He did know that he wanted his own organization to have an absolutely clean record. Malcolm decided that a leader who preached morality and preached a religious way of life should start with himself as an example.

Malcolm, while he was with the Nation of Islam, had accumulated almost nothing in the way of financial gain. The profits from the newspaper he created, *Muhammad Speaks*, which was being sold throughout the country, went to the Nation of Islam. Even the royalties from the book he had agreed to publish with Doubleday were signed over to the Nation of Islam. For Malcolm to start the next phase of his life he had to go to Boston and talk to his sister Ella.

"Ella," he said, "I want to make the pilgrimage to Mecca."

One-sixth of all the people of the world follow the religion of Islam. It is the youngest of the three religions most widely followed in the West: Judaism, Christianity, and Islam. While it is not widely known in the United States, Islam is the dominant religion of Africa and Asia.

The basic belief of Muslims, those that follow Islam, can be summed up in one sentence: There is no god but God (Allah) and Muhammad is the prophet of God. There are five demands on those who follow the Islamic faith: They must confess that they are believers in Islam, they must worship through their five daily prayers, they must fast for the month of Ramadan, they must make a pilgrimage or *hajj* to Mecca, and they must demonstrate their generosity to the poor.

For Malcolm the *hajj* was both a symbol of religious devotion and of his break from the Nation of Islam. Most Nation of Islam members did not and would never be able to make the trip to Mecca. To begin with, the expense of the long trip to Mecca, in Saudi Arabia, was too much for most members. Second, to enter the Islamic holy city one had to receive permission from Islamic officials. The Nation of Islam, or the "Black Muslims," as they were called, were often not considered true Muslims by the international Islamic community.

Malcolm applied for a visa and was told that no Muslim who had converted to Islam in America could get a passport to the holy city without a letter of approval from Dr. Mahmoud Youssef Shawarbi, the director of the Federation of Islamic Associations in the United States. Malcolm had met Dr. Shawarbi previously, and it was with confidence that he called him. Dr. Shawarbi was glad to hear from Malcolm, and the needed letter of approval was quickly given. He also gave him a book, *The Eternal Message of Muhammad,* by Abd ar-Rahman Azzam, a Saudi scholar and an advisor of King Faisal, the ruler of Saudi Arabia. He also gave Malcolm the telephone number of the author's son who lived in Jedda, Saudi Arabia, and that of his own son.

On April 13, 1964, Malcolm's wife and three daughters accompanied him on the trip from his East Elmhurst home to nearby Kennedy Airport. The first stop of his flight was in Frankfurt, Germany, where Malcolm took a brief tour of the city before catching his next flight to Cairo. In his autobiography he states that he was struck by the friendliness of the German people he met in Frankfurt.

It was obvious that Malcolm, even before the trip, had made some very sweeping decisions about the philosophy of the Nation of Islam. He was soon referring to the Muslims as a separatist organization. In speeches he would make shortly after he returned from his trip he would announce that he was no longer restricted by the Muslims. Although he expressed a great deal of hurt in his split from Elijah Muhammad and the Nation of Islam it was clear that he was ready to move on.

The break between Malcolm and Elijah Muhammad was one that could have been predicted years before, and which Muhammad surely anticipated. Elijah Muhammad was basically a conservative man with a radical idea: the self-development of African-Americans apart from white Americans. He was willing to patiently create a movement that would slowly grow, and which would affect limited numbers of people for the time being. Malcolm was an enormously gifted man, a thinker, a man to whom the idea of revolution was not only possible, but necessary. He believed, as the writer Toni Cade Bambara stated, that the ultimate goal of a black leader was to make revolution irresistible.

Muhammad understood young men. He could sense Malcolm's impatience, and his need for guidance and reassurance in his early days with the Nation of Islam. Muhammad also saw that Malcolm was not a man whose ideas and ambitions would be held in check forever. Malcolm's effect on the press was also understood. He was a dynamic speaker. His appearance, his six-foot-three-inch height, his boyish smile, his quiet theatrics, kept the cameras rolling. Muhammad saw all of this, saw the lure of the spotlight, and realized its dangers. But Malcolm had been expanding the Nation of Islam at a great rate. Muhammad hoped he could contain the younger, more gifted, man.

Malcolm's sense of self was both effective and, to many, annoying. Some saw his comments on what he was doing as manipulative and mocking; others saw them as demonstrations of his openness. But his self-awareness, the keen sense of who he was as a black man, allowed Malcolm to grow at an enormous rate. When he broke from the Nation of Islam, Malcolm knew he needed even more growth. He needed to see more, to talk more with people with a wider world view, and without the restrictions that the philosophy of the Nation of Islam placed upon him. He needed, he said, to start thinking for himself. In truth, he had always thought for himself, but had tried to fit his thinking into the concept of the Nation of Islam and Elijah Muhammad.

What neither man knew, though, was the extent to which they were both being watched by local police and the F.B.I. Malcolm suspected that many of his conversations were being reported to government organizations. F.B.I. reports detailed private conversations between Elijah Muhammad and his staff about the fact that Malcolm had left their organization. Years later it would be discovered that

Malcolm X in Egypt

both the Nation of Islam and the Moslem Mosque, Incorporated, had been infiltrated by police and F.B.I. informants.

Undercover police officer Gene Roberts would later testify that his first assignment was to infiltrate the Muslims.

Malcolm took a United Arab Airlines flight from Frankfurt to Cairo where he spent two days sightseeing and thinking. Malcolm was greeted warmly in Cairo, and through the influence of a man he had met on the plane, he joined a group of Muslim pilgrims who, like him, were making the pilgrimage to Mecca.

The trip to Mecca, for people first coming into Saudi Arabia, begins in the city of Jedda. On the plane into the coastal city there was an air of expectation as the pilgrims, dressed in the traditional covering of white cloths, one about the waist and the other over the shoulder, began the most important journey of their lives.

There were thousands upon thousands of pilgrims at Jedda, of all races and all colors. In a way Malcolm felt part of the huge mass of humanity: He was the same color, or lighter, than most of them. But he didn't know the rituals that they knew, and when they chanted Islamic prayers he didn't know them. Malcolm decided to watch, and to learn. He was assigned to a group of pilgrims and a guide who was to be responsible for them. Malcolm's group approached the officials who inspected the passports and belongings of the pilgrims. His American passport was examined, as was his letter of permission from Dr. Shawarbi. It was not sufficient. Despite the pleas of the Muslims who were with his group, Malcolm was told that he had to go before the Muslim high court, the *Mahgama Sharia*, for final approval.

The pilgrimage to Mecca is a religious privilege not taken lightly by the Islamic world. It is not a journey to be taken by sightseers or those who are not truly Muslims.

Because it was Friday night, the Islamic sabbath, Malcolm had to wait until the next day to appeal to the court.

He was taken to a place to rest. There were other Muslims there. At prayer times he was embarrassed because he did not know either Arabic or the Islamic rituals. He was a Muslim minister in the United States, without knowing the fundamentals of his own religion. Malcolm worried that he would be refused the needed permission. Then he remembered that he had the telephone number of Abd ar-Rahman Azzam's son.

Still unsure of himself, he went to a man who looked like an official and asked him to make a telephone call to the author's son. The official complied, and in an amazingly short time the man, the son of an author of a book on the Islamic religion, had come to get Malcolm. Soon they were on their way to the city of Jedda where Malcolm was put up in a luxury hotel.

Malcolm was learning about the world of Islam, but he was learning something else: that he was well-known and respected throughout the world.

The men who showed Malcolm this hospitality were Muslims, and they were white. They talked to Malcolm about his conversion, and about his racial attitudes. There is a saying in the Islamic faith that one cannot be a true Muslim unless he wishes for his brother what he wishes for himself, and Malcolm was asked if he really felt that all white men were devils.

Malcolm explained that in Saudi Arabia the term "white" was merely a description of a person's color, while in the United States it often reflected racist ideas, such as the superiority of one race over another. When signs were put on drinking fountains, noting that one was for "white" people and the other for "colored," or "Negroes," they were really saying that people of color were not good enough to drink from the same fountains as whites.

The racial problems in Europe and North America were well known in other parts of the world, especially in those areas in which there were people of color. Saudi Arabia was a country which had people of all colors, many of whom were as dark as or darker than Malcolm.

In the morning Malcolm was taken before the judge and questioned about the sincerity of his beliefs. Malcolm was completely open, and answered the questions carefully. At the end of the questioning, he was recognized as a true Muslim.

"I hope you will become a preacher of Islam in America," he was told.

With that, Malcolm's name was entered into the Holy Register at Jedda.

That evening he was driven to Mecca. Malcolm Little, the son of a Baptist minister, the teenage burglar, formerly the leading voice of the Nation of Islam in America, was about to make the final conversion to Islam.

There were tens of thousands of pilgrims, from all over the world. They were of all colors, from blue-eyed blonds to black-skinned Africans. But we were all participating in the same ritual, displaying a spirit of unity and brotherhood that my experiences in America had led me to believe never could exist between the white and the non-white.

—The Autobiography of Malcolm X

The pilgrimage to Mecca is not simple. To be lawful, the pilgrim must wear only the traditional covering, must stand in Arafat, twelve miles from Mecca, and circle the sacred black stone in the Kaaba in the court of the Great Mosque. In addition, the pilgrim must spend time in Al Muzdalifa, run between the hills of Safa and Marwah, and perform other rituals. Malcolm, with the help of his Muslim guide, performed the rituals, and made the sacred *hajj* that only a small percentage of Muslims are privileged to make.

Malcolm spent some time in Saudi Arabia as the guest of King Faisal. He was surprised that his hosts were as eager to talk to him as he was to them. People from all over the world asked him what was going on in America, and why blacks were suffering so. The news from back home told of riots in New York City, Jersey City, and Detroit. What would happen to the great Western country? they asked.

Malcolm said that it depended on what Americans learned from the riots.

Malcolm flew to Beirut, Cairo, Lagos, and Accra. He was astonished at how many people not only recognized him,

A meeting with King Faisal of Saudi Arabia

but had listened to his speeches. As he traveled, he encountered people of all kinds and all races, many who had proven themselves as fighters against oppression of any kind. Malcolm spoke at universities, to small groups of government officials, to American expatriates, and to Peace Corps workers. He spoke to whites as well as blacks; with the ambassador from Mali; the daughters and widow of Richard Wright, the black American writer; and with Kwame Nkrumah, President of Ghana. A state dinner was held in his honor by the Chinese ambassador to Ghana.

Part of Malcolm's trust for these people, his growth, was his new willingness to accept people as individuals. He had always accepted blacks as individuals, understanding that some were race-conscious and fighters for human rights for all people, while others were busy emulating whites to the detriment of other blacks. But for a long time he had not accepted whites. Now he knew he must change.

Malcolm X in a mosque

14

♦

A New
Message

MALCOLM took a new name, El Hajj Malik el Shabazz. He returned to the United States on a Pan Am flight from Paris on the twenty-first of May. He arrived at four twenty-five in the afternoon, and his wife met him with their daughters and a few followers. It was hardly the same Malcolm whom they had known before, clearly not the same Malcolm who had helped to build the temple in Detroit nearly a dozen years before.

When he had been with the Nation of Islam, he had

expanded that organization to build a larger base of African-American activists than had ever been assembled before. But now that he had left the Nation of Islam and had spoken to African and Asian leaders, now that he had gained the attention of so many people of color around the world, Malcolm had become, potentially, the most dangerous man in America. His speeches were a call to arms.

> *The newly awakened people all over the world pose a problem for what is known as Western interests, which are imperialism, colonialism, racism, and all these other negative isms, or vulturistic isms. Just as the external forces pose a grave threat, they can see that the internal forces pose an even greater threat.*

By this time the F.B.I. was monitoring his phone calls, his travel arrangements, and speeches. Paid informants reported on his private conversations. Gene Roberts, a black undercover agent who would later use his color to infiltrate the Black Panthers for the F.B.I., attended his meetings.

Malcolm had a new message that he needed to get out. Two days after he arrived at Kennedy Airport he announced, in a debate with journalist Louis Lomax, that he had changed his mind about whites. And shortly after, in Chicago, he stated that he would be willing to work with white groups if he felt that they were sincere in their efforts to help African-Americans gain a full measure of freedom.

Malcolm repeated his theme of creating a worldwide bond of black people. He claimed, in a letter to the *Am-*

sterdam News, that Pan-Africanism would accomplish for people of African descent what Zionism had done for Jews all over the world. It would give blacks from the United States, from Ghana, Nigeria, Mali, South Africa, Brazil, Cuba, and all the countries where blacks found themselves, a spiritual bond that would be a source of identity and strength.

The formation of the Muslim Mosque, Incorporated, had been Malcolm's response to his break with the Nation of Islam. Now he wanted an organization that had a more international purpose, and on the twenty-eighth of June, 1964, Malcolm announced the formation of the Organization of Afro-American Unity. The tenets of the new organization were considered at great length and carefully written. They represented a major shift in Malcolm's thinking.

I — Establishment
The Organization of Afro-American Unity shall
include all people of African descent in the West-
ern Hemisphere, as well as our brothers and
sisters on the African Continent.

While the teachings of the Nation of Islam indicated that all peoples of African descent were brothers and sisters and participants in the struggle for justice, Malcolm's Pan-Africanist view took the teachings a major step forward by announcing that the organization was established specifically to unify Africans on an international basis.

It is also interesting that Malcolm worded the declaration to include Africans, and not just "black Africans."

The first meeting of the Organization of Afro-American Unity

Another indication of Malcolm's changing philosophy lies in the preamble to the charter of the Organization of Afro-American Unity:

> *Resolved to reinforce the common bond of purpose between our people by submerging all of our differences and establishing a non-religious and non-sectarian constructive program for human rights.*

As national minister for the Nation of Islam, Malcolm had carried out a policy in which the Nation of Islam did not participate with other groups in civil rights activities or protests. In this new document, he announced that he was willing to put aside differences between his new group, the Organization of Afro-American Unity, and other black groups. He began to work feverishly to build up the organization.

He would not, however, be working with Elijah Muhammad.

Muhammad Speaks, the newspaper that Malcolm had established as the voice of the Nation of Islam, began to print articles against him. They accused him of betraying Elijah Muhammad, and of never having believed in his message. It was pointed out that to accuse falsely a Muslim of adultery was a sin.

Malcolm kept getting death threats. When he appeared on radio call-in shows, anonymous callers would say that he was going to be "bumped off," and that he was "as good as dead."

The calls came to his home as well, even when he had his number unlisted.

Malcolm told Alex Haley that he had helped form the Nation of Islam and knew what its members could do and what they couldn't do. He indicated that the Muslim organization did not have the ability to do that kind of spying. He suspected that there was a government agency somehow involved in the threats, and began to mistrust people in his organization.

In July, Malcolm returned to Africa and attended the Organization of African Unity in Cairo. He was the only American allowed to attend the conference and submitted a paper in which he asked the delegates to consider the plight of the twenty million African-Americans in the United States. Again, it was noted by American observers that Malcolm had full access to the African delegates when other Americans were not allowed into the meetings. Malcolm was clearly being welcomed in Africa.

Alexandria, in the north of Egypt, looks more like a European than an African city. The Roman influence is still very much present, and the inhabitants are well-educated and cosmopolitan. Malcolm spoke to over six hundred Muslim students representing seventy-three Asian and African nations at a banquet given by the Supreme Council of Islamic Affairs. In Addis Ababa he spoke to five hundred students.

Malcolm realized that his best chance to create a really lasting organization would be to get the support of African leaders, something he thought he could do. Malcolm arranged conferences with Jomo Kenyatta, President of Kenya, and Milton Obote, President of Uganda.

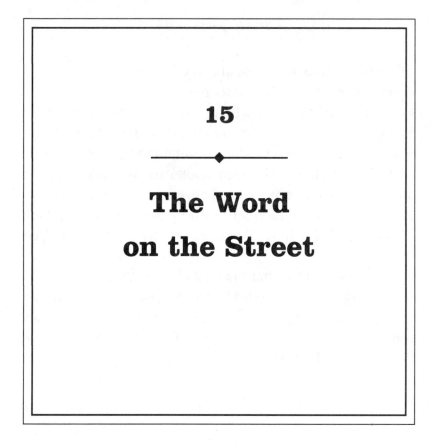

15

◆

The Word
on the Street

J OMO KENYATTA, of the Kikuyu people in Kenya, was
already in his seventies when Malcolm met him but
had been one of the early supporters of African unity. He
had been imprisoned for years in Kenya for leading the
feared Mau Mau movement.

Milton Obote had led his country to independence and
was also in favor of African unity.

Some African leaders were particularly interested in
what pressures could be brought to bear on world orga-

nizations to support the development of African countries below the Sahara, many of which had been recently freed from colonialism. These leaders also realized that African-Americans, if represented as a group, would form, by far, the richest African country in the world.

By the middle of October, Malcolm had met with eleven heads of state in Africa, returning to the United States on Tuesday, the twenty-fourth of November, 1964. After meeting with the members of his Organization of Afro-American Unity, Malcolm held a press conference at the airport.

He said that he had gathered support for an appeal to the United Nations on behalf of African-Americans. He said that the United States had violated the human rights of African-Americans.

The F.B.I. had reported on Malcolm's security arrangements, saying that "approximately fifteen to twenty MMI [Muslim Mosque, Incorporated] members are expected to guard Malcolm X upon his arrival."

Malcolm, in breaking with the Nation of Islam, had made many enemies within it and among some militant groups who resented the idea that Malcolm had now declared his willingness to work with all groups, including the more moderate ones. But he was also attracting a great deal of support from the members of the black middle class who had been put off by the Nation of Islam. Many professional writers were willing to help him put together a program, and to help with organizational work. Other groups were approaching Malcolm, and he regarded them cautiously.

Malcolm had been considered important enough by this time to be the subject of major magazine interviews and articles. The *Saturday Evening Post* did a long article on Malcolm toward the end of 1964, more or less synopsizing the *Autobiography* that was being written by Alex Haley.

In February a second statement was issued from the Organization of Afro-American Unity. It contained another surprise:

> *We Afro-Americans feel receptive toward all peoples of goodwill. We are not opposed to multi-ethnic associations in any walk of life. In fact, we have had experiences which enable us to understand how unfortunate it is that human beings have been set apart or aside from each other because of characteristics known as "racial" characteristics.*

There follows in the statement a rather long-winded explanation of why the Organization of Afro-American Unity must be exclusively for people of African descent, but it is clear that Malcolm was saying that he was willing to work with whites.

One reason for Malcolm's break with the Nation of Islam was his disappointment with his former friend and mentor, Elijah Muhammad. Malcolm had made a series of public statements about Elijah Muhammad, whose philosophy he had seemingly agreed with such a short time before. But Malcolm's dissatisfaction started long before his actual break with Elijah Muhammad. While still working under the banner of the Nation of Islam he had grown away from its principles.

Malcolm wrote an open letter to Elijah Muhammad, suggesting that the two men forget their differences and work toward their common goals. Malcolm had made both public and private offers of peace to Elijah Muhammad, and Elijah Muhammad did make a statement that he would be willing to forgive Malcolm, but no reconciliation took place. Both of these leaders were still getting mysterious death threats.

Malcolm was taking a dangerous course, and he knew it. He felt that at least some of the death threats against him did come from members of the Nation of Islam. It didn't matter if Elijah Muhammad had sanctioned the threats or not; if someone wanted to harm him, it could still happen.

The word on the streets of Harlem was somber. Malcolm, it was said, was marked for death.

16

The Assassination

To come right down to it, if I take the kind of things in which I believe, then add to that the kind of temperament that I have, plus the one hundred per cent dedication I have to whatever I believe in — these are ingredients which make it just about impossible for me to die of old age.
—The Autobiography of Malcolm X

SOMETIMES a certain kind of rumor bounces around the streets of Harlem, making its way from stoop to street corner, from corner bar to barbershop, even to church basements where portly matrons admonish younger members not to repeat it. It's not the kind of rumor shouted from the pavement to second-story windows, but the kind that is solemnly whispered. It is more than rumor, it is the word on the street. In February, 1965, the word on the street was that Malcolm was going to be killed.

In February, Malcolm had four children. His wife was pregnant with twin girls, Malikah and Malaak, who would be born the following fall. The morning of the fourteenth of February was cold. Malcolm was asleep. His oldest daughters were asleep in one bedroom, and his youngest daughter slept in the bedroom opposite Malcolm and Betty's. Something woke Malcolm, perhaps a noise, a feeling, as he lay in the darkness. Startled, he sprang up from where he lay. There was the sound of broken glass, and Malcolm called to his wife. The living room was on fire! Malcolm and Betty Shabazz gathered their children and ran out the back door.

The first fire engines arrived at the Queens house at ten minutes to three. The firemen put the fire out. The fire marshals the next day found that the bushes in front of Malcolm's house were scorched, as were the Venetian blinds that covered the broken rear window. There were broken bottles, some scorched, in various parts of the house. Gasoline had been used in the front room and there was a bottle of gasoline in the rear bedroom where Malcolm's older daughters slept.

The day after Malcolm X's house was firebombed

The F.B.I. report said that one of the investigators felt that Malcolm had an idea of who set the fire, and that he had tried to frighten off the culprit with a pistol that misfired.

Malcolm was badly shaken, and it was the opinion of the investigator that he needed medical help. A doctor was called and Malcolm was sedated. The sedative made him drowsy, and he slept most of the rest of the day.

Later that evening, in Detroit, he apologized to his audience for his drowsiness.

C. Eric Lincoln, in 1961, published a book, *The Black Muslims in America*. Lincoln had been hostile to the Muslim movement but had brought about a great deal of understanding of the forces that created the movement. But now, with Malcolm divorced from the Nation of Islam, Lincoln had drawn closer to him. He asked Malcolm to come up to Brown University and talk to the students there.

"I tell you, Professor Lincoln, I may be dead on Tuesday," Malcolm said.

"Come on, Malcolm, cut the bull . . . t," Dr. Lincoln said. "Come on up and talk to these kids."

When Dr. Lincoln realized that Malcolm was serious, he asked him why he didn't go to the police.

"They already know it . . ." Malcolm answered.

The Audubon Ballroom had been a vital part of the Harlem scene for decades. The big black bands had all appeared there, rallies had been organized there, dances and black-tie affairs held there were reported on by the local press. On the fifteenth of February Malcolm had spoken to nearly six hundred people at the Audubon. On the twenty-first of February, less than a week later, he was scheduled to speak again. Malcolm was still building the Organization of Afro-American Unity, testing his ideas in this public forum, offering what he believed to be a new and vital vision to his people. It would be a vision that he could direct without the restricting concepts of the Nation of Islam and that organization's built-in limitations.

Malcolm had heard the word on the street, he had heard the mocking phone calls that came to his house despite his unlisted number. He kept an automatic rifle fully loaded and ready to use in self-defense. He checked the doors to make sure they were locked. He peered cautiously into

With rumors and death threats flying, Malcolm X began keeping a loaded gun for self-defense.

the streets outside the Hotel Theresa where he was staying. These were streets he knew well, had walked down hundreds of times as a teenager, had spoken on as a man. Now they were streets to be feared.

Malcolm, knowing that any speech, any meal, any minute, might be his last, vowed to go on. Even going to the Audubon to speak to a crowd of followers who had come to hear him would be a risk, he knew.

It was a fairly mild February afternoon. Black women in their wide Sunday hats, Bibles under their arms, headed home from Christian church services. Children played on the street. Outside the Audubon police had put up barriers to control the expected crowds. In a backstage dressing room Malcolm paced nervously, his mind torn between what he would say to the gathered audience and the hundreds of other pieces of business associated with the building of an organization.

The audience filed in slowly, making their way down the side aisles into the folding chairs that covered the dance floor. Many of the women, in modest Islamic tradition, wore long dresses. Friends greeted friends; there was a mention of the amount of police in front of the ballroom.

Shortly before 3:00 P.M., Benjamin X took the microphone and greeted the audience. At about 3:05, Malcolm came out on the stage. He gave the Muslim greeting:

"As-salaam alaikem."

The greeting was returned by the audience. *"Wa-alaikem salaam."* His voice was calm, deliberate. Malcolm began his speech:

"Brothers and Sisters."

There was a stillness in the audience as Malcolm's voice, clear and reassuring, started his message.

"Get your hand out my pocket!" a man wearing a three-quarter-length black leather coat jumped to his feet and yelled at the man next to him.

Angry words were exchanged. Malcolm raised his hand and stepped from behind the podium, trying to calm things down. Two security guards rushed toward the two men.

Suddenly the man who had stood first pulled something from inside his coat. The audience began to scatter.

"Watch out! Watch out!"

There was a series of shots in rapid order, and then a booming noise. Chairs were flying everywhere, people were screaming. Betty Shabazz was sitting in the front row. Her girls were wearing snowsuits and she was trying to take them off when she heard the commotion. She pulled her children to her and tried to cover their bodies with her own.

"There's a bomb! There's a bomb!"

There were two men in front of Malcolm, and one of them was firing a pistol. Two other men were firing from the side, one with a sawed-off shotgun. Malcolm's guards began to fire back. People were crawling along the floor, trying to stay out of the crossfire. Men were lying over the bodies of their wives, trying to protect them.

In the lobby, a man with a forty-five rushed toward the stairs, firing indiscriminately. One of Malcolm's followers slammed into him, knocking him down the stairs. The forty-five fell from the man's hand as he tried to grab the banister for support. There was a scramble for the loose gun, and Malcolm's man got to it first and tried to fire it. Nothing. Reuben X, one of Malcolm's bodyguards, fired a shot at one of the two men who had started the distraction in the first place, and hit him in the leg.

Outside the ballroom, police and passersby were startled as the crowd began to rush into the street. People pointed to a man with a gun and he was wrestled to the ground. He was being punched and kicked as the police tried to prevent him from being killed. Reporters pushed through the crowd to phone in their stories.

Inside the Audubon a small gathering of people were on the stage. Some of them were crying. Betty Shabazz approached the still body of her husband. She was hoping . . . hoping . . . but in her heart she already knew the worst.

A Japanese woman who had brought her son to hear the speech cradled Malcolm's head in her hands. Some-one asked if anybody had called for an ambulance.

Between the living, frozen for the moment in shock and

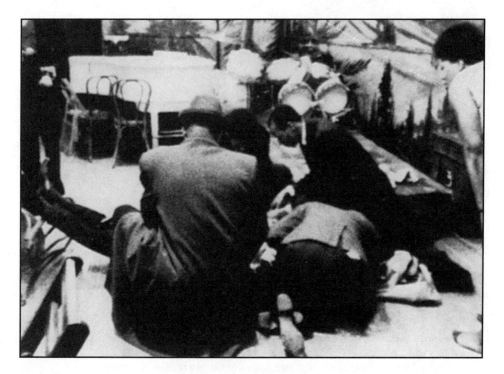

Malcolm X lies wounded

grief, lay Malcolm. The white shirt was opened by dark fingers looking to help. The holes, dark in their grim pattern within the spreading stain, caused the hand to recoil.

Gene Roberts, the undercover policeman, came to the stage. Lifting Malcolm's face to his, he tried to give him mouth-to-mouth resuscitation. The kiss of life came much too late. The people on the stage of the Audubon began to turn away, each to his or her own anguish. Malcolm was dead.

The police carrying the murdered Malcolm X's body from the Audubon Ballroom

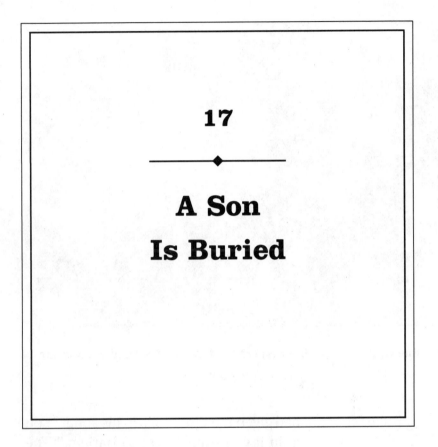

17

A Son
Is Buried

SATURDAY MORNING, the twenty-seventh of February, 1965. In Harlem the first light of day came grudgingly. Tenements that had been huddled in the grim darkness of mourning now emerged like geometric specters against the cold gray sky. There was a stillness about the streets. People spoke in whispers.

It was cold. Bone chillingly cold. Catch your breath and pull your collar tightly around your neck cold, but already the mourners had begun to line up for Malcolm's funeral.

The line of people paying respect to Malcolm X wound around the block.

Duke Ellington had given the directions in his song: "You must take the A train if you want to get to Harlem." The A train stopped at 145th Street and Eighth Avenue. From there it was a short walk to the Faith Temple Church of God on 147th and Amsterdam.

Dan Watts, Malcolm's friend and advisor, noticed how many older women were standing in the lines to take one last look at this son of Harlem.

There were hundreds of police inside and outside of the church. People had never seen so many black policemen. On either side of Betty Shabazz, Malcolm's widow, stood a black plainclothes detective.

Malcolm's body lay wrapped in the traditional white winding cloth of his faith. Beneath the glass shield of the casket he seemed so very distant. In death there was no sign of the youthfulness that had been so much a part of his living charm.

The funeral was simple. Ossie Davis and his wife, Ruby Dee, read messages of condolence. Ossie delivered the eulogy. He spoke of Malcolm as the manhood of black America. Then the casket was closed, and the procession to the cemetery began.

Betty Shabazz at the burial site

18

◆

Who Killed Malcolm?

A T THE SCENE of the murder, the police had captured a man named Talmadge Hayer. A few days later, Norman 3X Butler and Thomas 15X Johnson, both identified as being part of the Nation of Islam, were also arrested. The police investigation continued. There were eyewitnesses to the assassination who identified the three shooters, but the detectives working on the case did not believe that they had acted on their own. Someone had arranged to have Malcolm murdered.

The accused (left to right): Norman 3X Butler, Thomas 15X Johnson, and Talmadge Hayer

At the trial there was a parade of witnesses who testified as to what had happened that day in the Audubon Ballroom. The three defendants pled not guilty, ridiculing the prosecutor's accusations.

Hayer testified that he had found the .45 caliber pistol that had his fingerprints on it, that he had decided to keep it, and was on his way out of the ballroom when someone mistakenly accused him of the murder. He said that he was not in the Nation of Islam.

Butler said that he didn't know anything about the murder, that he had not been at the ballroom.

Johnson said that he had stayed home all day, that he had never handled a rifle.

As the case progressed Hayer changed his story. He said

179

that he had actually been part of the assassin team, and had fired at Malcolm, but that Butler and Johnson had not been there.

"Who were the others?" the prosecutor asked.

Hayer said that he wouldn't reveal their names. He said that he had been hired by someone.

"Who hired you?" the prosecutor asked.

Hayer said that he wouldn't reveal that, either. He refused to reveal how much money he had been offered.

On March eleventh, 1966, Hayer, Norman 3X Butler, and Thomas 15X Johnson were all found guilty of murder in the first degree. On the fourteenth of April, they were all sentenced to life imprisonment. The three men would not become eligible for parole until late 1991.

Who killed Malcolm and why? There were theories. Some said that it was the Nation of Islam, worried that Malcolm's new organization would threaten its existence. Others said that it was a government plot, that Malcolm's visits to international leaders posed a threat to the American social order.

There are always theories about why black men who speak up for their people are killed or imprisoned.

Malcolm understood this. He was not surprised that Marcus Garvey had been imprisoned, and then deported. There were theories that Garvey was embezzling money from his organization, that he was participating in a stock fraud.

Malcolm was not surprised that his father, Earl Little, had been killed, or at the mystery surrounding his death. He might have been surprised to know that the F.B.I. had correspondence in their files from his father concerning Garvey.

He was not surprised that Medgar Evers had been killed, or that his killer was never brought to justice.

He would not have been surprised that Martin Luther King, Jr., was killed, or at the mysteries surrounding his death.

He would not have been surprised about the death of Fred Hampton of the Black Panthers, or even that the same man who had infiltrated the Organization of Afro-American Unity would one day infiltrate the Panthers.

In an interview with journalist Claude Lewis in December, 1964, Malcolm said:

> *You'll find very few people who feel like I feel that live long enough to get old. I'll tell you what I mean and why I say that. When I say by any means necessary, I mean it with all my heart, and my mind and my soul. But a black man should give his life to be free, but he should also be willing to take the life of those who want to take his. It's reciprocal. And when you think like that you don't live long . . .*

19

The Legacy

WHO was Malcolm X, and what is his legacy?
Malcolm's life seems so varied, he did so many
things over the far too short thirty-nine years of his life,
that it almost appears that there was not one Malcolm at
all, but four distinct people. But in looking at Malcolm's
life, in examining the expectations against what he actually
did, we see a blending of the four Malcolms into one dynamic personality that is distinctively American in its

character. For only a black man living in America could have gone through what Malcolm went through.

The first Malcolm was Malcolm the child, who lived in Nebraska and Michigan. He lived much like a million other black boys born in the United States. He was loved by two parents, Earl and Louise Little. From them he learned about morality, and decency, and the need to do well in school. His parents gave him a legacy of love, but also a legacy of pride.

Malcolm saw his father, a Baptist minister, at the meetings of the Universal Negro Improvement Association, saw him speaking about the black race, and about the possibility of justice. From what the young Malcolm saw, from what he experienced as a young child, one might have expected him, upon reaching maturity, to become a religious man and an activist for justice, as was his father.

Even when Earl Little was killed, Louise Little tried to hold the family together. Malcolm started school and did well. His mother saw to it that he did his assignments, and there was no doubt that Malcolm was bright. Bright children often understand their gifts, and it is possible that Malcolm understood his early on. He said in his autobiography that he had not given a lot of thought to what he wanted to do with those gifts when he was asked by a teacher in the eighth grade. A lawyer, he ventured.

Malcolm had not known exactly what he wanted to do with his talents, but he understood that the talents he possessed were valued in his schoolmates. The teacher said to him that it was not practical for him to be a lawyer, because he was black. The teacher probably thought of himself as being a realist. There is no use misleading Malcolm, he probably thought. Where does a black teenaged boy go, to what does he turn if he is not allowed the same avenues of value as his white friends?

The second Malcolm answers that question. The black teenager goes among his own people, and searches among the values of his peers for those he can use. So Malcolm bought the zoot suit, with the gold chain dangling against the pants leg. He bought the wide-brimmed hat and learned the hip jargon of the street, the same way teenagers today buy the gold chains and sneakers that cost enough to feed a family for a week. Malcolm was a human being, and human beings need to be able to look into the mirror and see something that pleases them. What had value in the American society that Malcolm knew? The conk had value, burning your hair until it was tortured enough to approximate the appearance of a white man's hair.

Malcolm said that he wanted to be a lawyer, to use his mind. He was told that no, he couldn't do that because he was black. Perhaps it wouldn't have made any difference what the teacher had said. As was the case with so many black teenagers, Malcolm's family, now with only the mother to support it, would not have been able to afford college for him.

Malcolm toughened himself. Malcolm used his mind. If he couldn't use it to study law, he would use it in street hustles. He used it in making money the way people in the inner cities who don't have "downtown" jobs make money. Eventually he used it to commit burglaries. Some societies never learn that to make a person socially re-

Malcolm X preaching, surrounded by the Fruit of Islam

185

sponsible you must first include him or her in your society. Malcolm's career as a petty criminal, much sensationalized in the autobiography he never got to read, ended quickly when he was caught, tried, and sentenced to eight to ten years in prison.

The second Malcolm, the one using his wits to survive on the streets, skirting both sides of the law, might have continued after he was released if it were not for the Nation of Islam. Elijah Muhammad claimed that he lifted Malcolm up and saved him from a life of degradation. Nothing was more truthful. The Nation of Islam, with its strict moral codes, its religion, its understanding, forgiveness, and even celebration of black men who had fallen by the wayside, was the garden from which the third Malcolm emerged.

Here now was Malcolm the religious man, the activist, the thinker, the man who stood up for his people, who confronted the forces of injustice in America at a time when black people were being beaten in the streets, were being publicly humiliated and even killed. Here was a Malcolm who offered himself as the voice of the defeated, the manliness of a people who badly needed manliness.

And he was a worker. He organized and preached. He cajoled and threatened. He attacked racism with the biting tone of the absolute cynic, vowing to attain freedom by any means necessary and with any sacrifice. He understood, as few other leaders did, that there were people like himself in the streets, and in the prisons, who had contributions to make. He included people in the struggle for human rights in America who had never before been included. This was the third Malcolm.

Malcolm grew. He grew away from the Nation of Islam,

and away from the separatist philosophy of that organization. The Nation of Islam had returned to him the wings that had been taken from him because of his color, and Malcolm, the fourth Malcolm, found himself able to fly.

What one would have expected, or at least hoped for, on meeting the wide-eyed boy in the Pleasant Grove Elementary School, was that he would one day touch the edge of greatness. It is what we wish for all children. The fourth Malcolm — the one with his head slightly bowed as he listened to Jomo Kenyatta, the great African leader, the one learning firsthand about the liberation of the African continent so that he could liberate his own — had touched the edge of that greatness.

Malcolm's life was about growth, about the intensely changing man that moved from thievery to honesty, from being a racial separatist to searching for true brotherhood, and from atheism to Islam.

But his life was also about the return to the idealism of his childhood. The world of the child, before he or she is exposed to racism, before he or she is conditioned to react to the hurts inflicted on him or her, is one of acceptance and love. Malcolm had grown, and in that growing had learned to accept those people, regardless of race or nationality, who accepted and loved him.

Malcolm spoke for the voiceless, for the people from whom not even some black leaders wanted to hear. He spoke for the jobless, and for the homeless. He spoke for the young men whose hard bodies, bodies that could perform miracles on inner-city basketball courts, were not wanted in America's offices. He spoke for the millions of black Americans who saw themselves as a minority in a world in which most of the inhabitants were people of color like themselves. He spoke for the men and women who had to turn too many other cheeks, had to fight off too many insults with nothing but smiles.

Malcolm had walked in their shoes, and they knew it when they heard him speak.

Thurgood Marshall, civil rights lawyer and, later, Supreme Court justice, understood the court system and the importance of having a legal basis for protest. He understood that for years racists and their supporters could simply hide behind the issue of legality, claiming that the only reason schools were segregated, the only reason housing was denied blacks, the only reason it was difficult to vote in certain places, was because of certain laws that had been on the books for years, and then work to prevent changes in the law.

Martin Luther King, Jr., knew the power of public persuasion. Racists and bigots wanted to look as if they were in the right. They wanted their families and friends to think that they were protecting southern women, or law and order, or even something as vague as a "way of life." He understood that nonviolence, in the wake of police dogs, and fire hoses, would attract a favorable world opinion of African-Americans.

But Malcolm, coming from the awareness of the Garvey tradition, and coming from the same street corners on which he would later "fish for the dead," having experienced the same hunger, the same frustrations, even the same jails as poor blacks did, understood something else as well: that all the goals of the mainstream civil rights movement, the civil rights laws, school integration, vot-

Spreading the word

ing rights, none of these would have meaning if African-Americans still thought of themselves as a racially crippled people, if they still walked with their heads down because they were black.

In the last year of his life, having grown away from the Nation of Islam, and having made a spiritual pilgrimage to Mecca, Malcolm was moving both to a new and an old place. He was moving more solidly into Pan-Africanism, the territory that his father had explored over forty years before.

Malcolm's message is remembered by many people who find comfort and inspiration in it today. One of them is the African-American poet Wopashitwe Mondo Eyen we Langa, who wrote the poem "Great Bateleur." A bateleur is a reddish-brown eagle found in Africa. It is notable for its acrobatic flying style and its ferocious cry as it dives to capture its prey.

Great Bateleur
(In Tribute to Malcolm)

We were pigeons, Malcolm
congregating at the park benches of America
to peck at the crumbs of America's wealth
but you were a bateleur
you did not coo at men's feet
gratefully bobbing your head for cast away scraps

We were wrens and sparrows
good survivors
good at nervous flight
from any sound and sight of fearsome threat

we could not
would not
hold our ground and fight
perhaps you feared like us
but you did not quiver
but thrust forward sharp talons boldly
yours were not the frantic chirpings
but the righteous clamor of indignation

We were ducklings waddling in shame
thinking ourselves ugly
seeking disguise in feathers that were foreign to us
but you hid yourself from no one
but smiled in the daylight
stretching your wings to soar

We were those who begged, Malcolm
who could not find courage
nor faith in ourselves
who could not peer into reflecting pools
nor look each other in the face
and see the beauty that was ours
but for you, Malcolm
but for you, Great Bateleur
Eagle of Africa
still your spirit flies.

Perhaps history will tell us that there were no wrong strategies in the civil rights movement of the sixties. That all factors involved, the pray-ins, the legal cases, the marches, the militancy, were all vital to the time, that each had its place. Undoubtedly, too, as current needs color memories of distant events, we will bring different concepts from that period of American history, and different voices. One voice that we will not forget is that of El Hajj Malik el Shabazz, the man we called Malcolm.

Chronology

	5/19/25	**Malcolm Little is born in Omaha, Nebraska.**
The stock market crashes to record lows. 10/29/29		
The Great Depression 1929–42	**9/28/31**	**Earl Little, Malcolm's father, is run over by a streetcar and dies in Lansing, Michigan. His death may have been caused by a white supremacist group.**
The Scotsboro case. Nine black boys are falsely accused and arrested for rape. 3/25/31		
	1938–41	**Malcolm lives in various foster homes in Lansing, Michigan.**
World War II 1939–45	**1/9/39**	**Louise Little, Malcolm's mother, is committed to a state mental hospital in Kalamazoo, Michigan.**
The Japanese attack Pearl Harbor, prompting the U.S. to enter World War II. 12/7/41	**2/41**	**Malcolm moves in with his sister Ella in Boston, Massachusetts.**

		3/43	**Moves to New York City.**
		2//27/46	**Begins serving prison term, for breaking and entering and armed robbery, at Charlestown State Prison.**
		1947–48	**Converts to the Nation of Islam while in prison.**
The Korean War	6/25/51– 7/27/53	**8/7/52**	**Paroled from prison. Moves to Detroit, Michigan.**
		8/31/52	**Hears Elijah Muhammad speak in Chicago, Illinois. Malcolm is given his X soon after.**
Brown v. Board of Education of Topeka ruling legally ends segregation in schools.	5/17/54	**6/54**	**Becomes minister of New York Temple Number Seven.**
Emmett Till kidnapped. Four days later, his body is found.	8/28/55		
Montgomery, Alabama, bus boycott begins	12/55		

		1/14/58	Marries Sister Betty X in Lansing, Michigan.
		11/58	Their first daughter, Attallah, is born.
Cuban revolution led by Fidel Castro.	1/1/59		
		12/60	Second daughter, Qubilah, is born.
		1962	Malcolm hears rumors concerning Elijah Muhammad.
		7/62	Third daughter, Ilyasah, is born.
		4/63	Meets with Elijah Muhammad in attempt to resolve their differences.
March on Washington, D.C.	8/28/63		
President John F. Kennedy assassinated.	11/22/63		
		12/1/63	Publicly comments on the Kennedy assassination and is "silenced" by the Nation of Islam.
		3/8/64	Split with the Nation of Islam announced in *The New York Times*.

3/16/64   **Forms new organization, Muslim Mosque, Inc.**

3/26/64   **Meets Martin Luther King, Jr.**

5/21/64   **Completes pilgrimage to Mecca. Returns as El Hajj Malik el Shabazz, with new ideals.**

6/28/64   **Announces formation of the secular Organization of Afro-American Unity.**

"Long, hot summer"   7/64–8/64
riots in various cities

Civil Rights Act of   7/2/64
1964 passed.

12/64   **Fourth daughter, Gamilah, is born.**

2/14/65   **House in Queens is firebombed.**

2/21/65   **Malcolm X is assassinated while delivering a speech in Harlem's Audubon Ballroom.**

Fall, 1965	**Twin daughters, Malaak and Malikah, are born.**
3/11/66	**Talmadge Hayer, Norman 3X Butler, and Thomas 15X Johnson are convicted of first degree murder in the shooting death of Malcolm X.**
4/14/66	**Hayer, Butler, and Johnson are sentenced to life imprisonment.**

Bibliography

———◆———

Books

Branch, Taylor. *Parting the Waters: America in the King Years 1954–63.* New York: Simon and Schuster, 1988.

Breitman, George. *The Last Year of Malcolm X: The Evolution of a Revolutionary.* New York: Pathfinder, 1967.

———. *Malcolm X Speaks.* New York: Grove Weidenfield, 1990.

Carson, Clayborne. *Malcolm X: The F.B.I. File.* New York: Carroll and Graf, 1991.

Clarke, John Henrik. *Malcolm X: The Man and His Times.* Trenton, NJ: Africa World Press, Inc., 1990.

———. *Marcus Garvey and the Vision of Africa.* New York: Vintage, 1974.

Cronon, E. D. *Black Moses: The Story of Marcus Garvey and The Universal Negro Improvement Association.* Madison: University of Wisconsin Press, 1968.

Gallen, David. *Malcolm X: As They Knew Him.* New York: Carroll and Graf, 1992.

Goldman, Peter. *The Death and Life of Malcolm X.* Chicago: University of Illinois Press, 1979.

Haley, Alex. *The Autobiography of Malcolm X.* New York: Ballantine, 1964.

Lincoln, C. Eric. *The Black Muslims in America.* Boston: Beacon Press, 1961.

Lipschutz, Mark R., and Rasmussen, R. Kent. *Dictionary of African Historical Biography.* Berkeley: University of California Press, 1978.

Lomax, Louis E. *When the Word Is Given.* New York: Signet Books, New American Library, 1963.

Muhammad, Elijah. *Message to the Blackman in America.* Newport News, VA: United Brothers Communications Systems, 1965.

Perry, Bruce. *Malcolm: The Life of a Man Who Changed Black America.* Barrytown, NY: Station Hill Press, 1991.

Newspapers

Negro World. May 22, June 19, July 3, 1926; January 29, February 5, February 19, 1927.

The New York Times. May 17, 1963; March 8, May 8, May 22, August 13, 1964; February 22, March 11, 1965.

Muhammad Speaks (various issues).

The State Journal (Lansing, MI). November 9, November 11, 1929; September 29, 1931.

Periodicals

The Black Scholar. "The Garveyite Parents of Malcolm X," by Ted Vincent, March/April, 1989.

Life, March 5, March 26, 1965.

Playboy interview, by Alex Haley, May, 1963.

Saturday Evening Post, September 12, 1964.

Acknowledgments

In preparing this book I am grateful to many people for their help, especially: Bertha Calloway, of the Great Plains Black Museum; Reginald Little; Robert Little; Dr. Tony Martin, of Brown University; and Dr. Betty Shabazz.

With special thanks to Rachel Gray/Scholastic, Inc. and Photo-Search Inc. for their photo research.

Photo Credits

Associated Press/Wide World Photos: pp. 61, 98, 117, 119, 124, 141, 154, 168, 173, 176, 177, 179.

The Bettmann Archive: p. 50.

Black Star: © John Launois, pp. 94, 149, 155; © Charles Moore, p. 118; © Sue Kellogg, p. 189.

Bostonian Society/Old State House: p. 35.

Culver Pictures: p. 52.

***Ebony* Magazine/Johnson Publishing Company:** pp. 112, 170.

The Federal Bureau of Investigation: p. 120.

Laurence Henry Collection, The Schomburg Center for Research in Black Culture, The New York Public Library, Astor, Lenox, and Tilden Foundations: pp. 86, 132.

The Louise Norton Little Family Foundation: p. 9.

Magnum Photos: © Eve Arnold, pp. 90, 137, 185; © Leonard Freed, p. 115; © Bruce Davidson, p. 131.

Massachusetts State Police: p. 59.

Michael Ochs Archives, used by permission of Dr. Betty Shabazz: p. 93.

Mr. Bab's Professional Photographer, Mason, Michigan: p. 33.

New York Daily News: pp. 126, 143.

Omaha-Douglas County Health Department: p. 13.

Pathfinder Press: © Robert Parent, p. 159.

Pleasant Grove Elementary School, Lansing Michigan: pp. 25, 27.

© **Richard Sanders:** p. 87.

The Schomburg Center for Research in Black Culture: pp. 19, 56, 65.

The Schomburg Center for Research in Black Culture, used by permission of Dr. Betty Shabazz: p. 38.

United Press International: pp. 30, 43, 174.

United Press International/The Bettmann Archive: pp. 71, 72.

Index

Page numbers for illustrations are in italics.